D1604243

FLAVORS of ALOHA

FLAVORS of ALOHA

COOKING WITH Tommy Bahama®

100 recipes

Recipes by Rick Rodgers, with text by Jeff Morgan

PHOTOGRAPHS BY PEDEN + MUNK

CHRONICLE BOOKS
SAN FRANCISCO

Published exclusively for Tommy Bahama by Chronicle Books LLC.

Tommy Bahama Book Development Team:
Terry R. Pillow, Chief Executive Officer
Rob Goldberg, Executive Vice President, Restaurants
Ferdinand van Alphen, Senior Vice President, Creative Services
Eric Karp, Director of Brand Marketing
Don Donley, Director of Culinary
Kyle Zitek, Director of Photography Production
Stennis Hirayama, Executive Chef, Mauna Lani
Kouri Killmeier, Executive Chef, New York City

Recipes and chefs' notes by Rick Rodgers
Introduction and essays by Jeff Morgan
Design by Toni Tajima
Prop styling by Amy Wilson
Food styling by Alison Attenborough
Assistant prop stylist: Nina Lalli
Assistant food stylists: Hadas Smirnoff, Julian Bolton, Dan Rosenzweig, and Petericia Ellis
Photography assistant: Jaesung Lee
Digital Technician: William Joos

Photos pages 104 and 112 per agreement with Parker Ranch, Waimea, Island of Hawaii. Founded in 1847, the 130,000-working cattle ranch is one of the largest cow and calf operations in the United States. A joint venture of Parker Ranch and Ulupono Initiative, the pasture-to-table enterprise Paniolo Cattle Company supports a growing demand for high-quality, affordable, locally raised Island beef.

Photos pages 187, 196, 205, 206, 208–209 per agreement with Greenwell Farms, Kealakekua, Island of Hawaii. Established in 1850, Greenwell Farms grows and operates its 100-percent Kona coffee processing on some of the most productive land in the Kona District and purchases freshly harvested coffee cherry from over 300 farmers in the North and South Kona regions. The farm is managed by fourth-generation farmers Tom and Jennifer Greenwell.

ISBN: 978-1-4521-4200-5

Manufactured in the United States.

This book has been set in FF Seria Sans by Martin Majoor.

10 9 8 7 6 5 4 3 2 1

Tommy Bahama
428 Westlake Avenue North, Suite 388
Seattle WA 98109
www.tommybahama.com

Chronicle Books LLC
680 Second Street
San Francisco CA 94107
www.chroniclebooks.com/custom

Tommy Bahama
MAKE LIFE ONE LONG WEEKEND™

CONTENTS

Foreword by Terry R. Pillow • 9

Introduction: A Feast for the Senses • 11

"THE HUMBLE FISHERMAN" ALAN KIRIU • 17

APPETIZERS AND PUPUS (STARTERS) 18

21 Crab Rangoon
22 Tommy's Famous Coconut Shrimp
25 Tuna Poke with Guacamole and Flatbread
26 Crispy Sriracha Shrimp
27 Lomi-Lomi Salmon with Tomatoes and Onions
30 Roasted Korean Chicken Wings
33 Maui Sweet Onion, Bacon, and Chive Dip
34 Pork Satay with Peanut Sauce
35 Minced Chicken in Lettuce Cups
36 Pork and Shrimp Gyoza
39 Spicy Sake Pickles
40 Spam Musubi

COOKING WITH THE ELEMENTS: EARTH • 43

SOUPS AND SALADS 44

45 Ono Oxtail and Greens Soup
46 Clam Soup with Shiitakes and Miso
48 Red Bean and Ham Soup
50 Mandarin Hot and Sour Soup
51 Tom Yum Shrimp Soup
53 Green Papaya and Shrimp Salad
54 Arugula, Fruit, and Goat Cheese Salad with Papaya Vinaigrette
57 Citrus and Hearts of Palm Salad with Kumquat Vinaigrette
58 Asian Slaw with Ginger Dressing
59 Romaine Hearts with Maui Onions and Carrot-Miso Dressing
62 Plate Lunch Potato-Macaroni Salad

HIRAYAMA FARMS, KAMUELA • 65

POULTRY 66

67 General Tso's Chicken
68 Chicken Katsu with Umami Sauce
71 Chicken Teriyaki with Grilled Shiitake Mushrooms
72 Chicken Yakitori
73 Chinese Roast Duck with Orange-Honey Glaze
76 Vietnamese Chicken Breasts with Savory Caramel Sauce
79 Chicken and Bacon Empanadas
80 Sweet and Sour Chicken with Mango and Asparagus
82 Kung Pao Chicken
83 Fried Chicken Mochiko
85 Grilled Chicken Bánh Mì

COOKING WITH THE ELEMENTS: WIND • 87

RED MEAT 88

89 Grilled Tamarind Short Ribs
90 Korean Steak with Ssamjang Dip
92 Braised Pork Belly in Steamed Buns
94 Guava-Glazed Baby Back Ribs
96 Pork Adobo
97 Roast Pork and Potatoes with Wine and Garlic Marinade
99 Kalua Pulled Pork Sandwiches
100 Lamb Shanks and Snap Peas with Red Curry Sauce
101 Huli Huli Pork Tenderloin and Pineapple with Old-School Teriyaki Marinade
102 Grilled Skirt Steaks with Kona Coffee Rub
105 Paniolo Beef and Vegetable Stew
107 Panko-Crusted Rack of Lamb with Green Onion Hoisin
108 Pork Burgers with Pineapple Chutney and Bacon

PARKER RANCH, WAIMEA • 113

SEAFOOD 114

115 Mahi Mahi with Macadamia Nut Crust and Papaya Salsa
116 Shrimp and Scallops in Thai Curry Sauce
118 Steamed Sea Bass with Ginger Dipping Sauce
121 Togarashi-Sesame Snapper with Sake and Lime Sauce
123 Salmon Fillets with Ginger Glaze
124 Grilled Swordfish with Orange-Miso Marinade
127 Ahi Tuna with Lemongrass Crust and Sweet Chili–Mustard Sauce
128 Portuguese Seafood and Sausage Stew

COOKING WITH THE ELEMENTS: FIRE • 133

NOODLES AND RICE 134

135 Chicken Chow Fun with Sugar Snap Peas and Shiitakes
136 Korean Cellophane Noodles with Chicken and Vegetables
141 Fried Rice with Kimchi, Bacon, and Peas
142 Garlic Fried Rice with Sausage, Eggs, and Green Onions
143 Chinatown Chow Mein with Pork and Mushrooms
144 Vietnamese Noodle Soup with Beef
147 Pan-Cooked Noodles with Shrimp and Chorizo (Pancit)
149 Saimin with Asian Chicken Broth
150 Pork Ramen with Shoyu Broth

HONAUNAU FARM, HONAUNAU-NAPOOPOO • 155

SIDE DISHES AND BREADS 156

157 Hawaiian-Style Rice
158 Cabbage and Daikon Kimchi
160 Drunken Mushrooms
161 Wasabi–Roasted Garlic Mashed Potatoes
162 Braised Baby Bok Choy with Macadamia Nuts
165 Sesame and Ginger Spinach
168 Asparagus with Oyster Sauce
169 Green Onion and Garlic Naan
170 Broccolini with Chile–Lemon Oil
172 Eggplant in Black Bean Sauce
175 Green Tea Rice with Peas
176 Portuguese Sweet Bread Rolls

COOKING WITH THE ELEMENTS: WATER • 179

DESSERTS 180

181 Jelly Malasadas
182 Chocolate Butter Mochi
183 Butter Mochi
184 Shave Ice with Fresh Fruit Syrups
186 Kona Coffee Flan
189 Mango, Raspberry, and Ginger Pie
190 Guava and Currant Tea Cake
193 Passion Fruit Chiffon Tart
194 Banana and Coconut Cream Meringue Pie
197 Macadamia Nut and Chocolate Toffee
199 Piña Colada Cake
203 Pineapple Crème Brûlée
204 Dobash Cake

GREENWELL FARMS, KEALAKEKUA • 207

COCKTAILS

29 Blue Hawaii
29 Cherry Blossom Martini
61 Pineapple Plantation
61 Tropical Itch
75 Zombie
75 Painkiller No. 2
138 Hibiscus Lime Cooler
138 Hibiscus Fizz
167 Singapore Sling
167 Mai Tai

Glossary • 211
Acknowledgments • 215
Index • 216

FOREWORD

AT TOMMY BAHAMA, the spirit of *aloha* has been our North Star since we opened our first store and restaurant nearly 20 years ago. The kind of hospitality, creativity, and thoughtfulness our restaurants offer embodies the *aloha* spirit. For years, locals and visitors alike have enjoyed our restaurants in Hawaii, and we are excited to share this book with you to bring the Tommy Bahama experience into your home.

The recipes in this book capture the essence of both Tommy Bahama and Hawaii—simple, flavorful, elegant, and fun. We've included some favorites straight from our restaurant menu along with Island staples that truly represent the essence of traditional Hawaiian cooking.

We believe that the art of cooking and the art of relaxation go hand in hand. In the spirit of our motto—"Make life one long weekend"—and *Flavors of Aloha*, we encourage you to kick back and take an "Island time" approach to cooking for family and friends, because everything tastes a little better when you're relaxed.

Mahalo,

Terry R. Pillow
Chief Executive Officer
Tommy Bahama

INTRODUCTION
A feast for the senses

HAWAII IS A FEAST FOR THE SENSES. Breathe in and smell the sweet spice that rises from hillside sugarcane. Rich soils, tropical sunshine, and blue skies make the land fertile, while the sea—never far away—bathes the coast in shimmering aquamarine. Surfing was invented here, and beneath the ocean waves swim the fish that have long provided sustenance to locals and visitors alike.

At Tommy Bahama, we have always revered Hawaii for its connection between culture, a sense of place, and its food. We aspire to create those same authentic connections in everything we do—from designing swimwear and clothing to creating accessories and gifts. Today, with Tommy Bahama restaurants throughout mainland America, Hawaii, and Japan, we also have a special connection to what we eat. And we want to share it with you.

This is the first in a series of *Cooking with Tommy Bahama* books. It's a mouthwatering collection of 100 recipes. Selected signature recipes for the Tommy Bahama restaurants, developed under the auspices of our Director of Culinary, Don Donley, have been adapted for this book. *Flavors of Aloha* tells the story of Hawaii through its food and the people who produce it. The Island community is home to indigenous Hawaiians and Asian and European immigrants. Together they have created a unique confluence of cultures: a panoply of cooking traditions. It's no wonder the art of the table has made Hawaii a culinary paradise—one that draws liberally from afar yet remains grounded in local custom.

Recipes pay homage to these diverse origins and include selections such as Tuna Poke with Guacamole and Flatbread, Steamed Sea Bass with Ginger Dipping Sauce, Guava-Glazed Baby Back Ribs, and Korean Steak with Ssamjang Dip. Desserts like Pineapple Crème Brûlée, Kona Coffee Flan, and Jelly Malasadas (Portuguese doughnuts) continue to seduce the palate at the end of dinner or as a midday treat.

In the pages that follow, you will also come to know the people who supply ingredients for great Island dining. They include longtime coffee farmer Tom Greenwell, cattle rancher Keoki Wood of Parker Ranch in Waimea, eco-farmer Steve Sakala of Honaunau EcoRetreat and Farm, and chef/farmer Stennis Hirayama, now executive chef at Tommy Bahama's Mauna Lani restaurant. Each of these talented individuals has a special relationship with the natural bounty of Hawaii. Their experience gives them an insider's understanding and perspective, which we are delighted to share with you.

We ask you to sit back, relax, and explore these pages at your leisure. The images are meant to inspire. They reflect a unique culture of dining and the provenance of what we eat. Our recipes are designed for home cooking. They are approachable and filled with natural, good-tasting ingredients grown as Nature intended. This book reflects the spirit of *aloha* (peace) and *ohana* (home). Ultimately, we hope to bring a sense of place to your dinner table, wherever it may be, with meals to nurture you, your friends, and family for years to come.

E'ai kākou! (Let's eat!)

When Alan Kiriu heads out to sea in his small, 18-foot fishing boat, the world is literally his oyster. "I'm just a humble fisherman who loves the serenity of the water," he says. Yet he is an integral part of an industry that is of major importance to Hawaii, for it provides both locals and visitors with the fresh-caught fish that are central to its cuisine.

The Hawaiian native works with basic materials: a rope, a hook, and a basket. That's how he catches tuna and mahi mahi. For really big fish, like the 700-pound marlin he once landed, he might use a rod and reel.

For part of the year, Alan also works as an accomplished special effects film technician. "I do the mechanical stuff," he explains, "like rain, explosions, and flipping cars" for such Hollywood blockbusters as the *Transformers* series. "My Hollywood friends gave me my nickname: Da Humble Fisherman."

Back on the water, Alan finds fishing gives him a thrill he can't match on screen. "It's dangerous out there," he reminds us. "You've got to be thinking about the wind and currents all the time. You have to be one with the sea."

He occasionally gets into trouble, like the time a fast-moving squall caught him off guard, and lightning hit his boat's antenna. "I felt it right through the steering wheel," he recalls matter-of-factly.

But clearly the benefits of a seafaring life outweigh the risks. Alan feeds his family with the freshest of fish. He delivers the rest of his catch from the back of his Toyota pickup to local restaurants like Tommy Bahama. "It's a simple life" he says, noting that his fast-paced Hollywood buddies are envious.

From the quiet of his boat, Alan is witness to a world few are privileged to know. At night, he can see plankton shimmering in the moonlight. And sometimes giant humpback whales swim so close he can look directly into their round, soulful eyes. "It's all so beautiful," he says. "I go with the flow, and I'm living the dream."

"THE HUMBLE FISHERMAN" ALAN KIRIU

APPETIZERS AND PUPUS (STARTERS)

The appetite-rousing snacks served before a Hawaiian meal are called pupus (a word that originally meant "snail"). These are usually served in a large array, with an assortment large enough for a meal designated as heavy pupus, and a smaller selection as light pupus.

21
CRAB RANGOON

22
TOMMY'S FAMOUS COCONUT SHRIMP

25
TUNA POKE WITH GUACAMOLE AND FLATBREAD

26
CRISPY SRIRACHA SHRIMP

27
LOMI-LOMI SALMON WITH TOMATOES AND ONIONS

30
ROASTED KOREAN CHICKEN WINGS

33
MAUI SWEET ONION, BACON, AND CHIVE DIP

34
PORK SATAY WITH PEANUT SAUCE

35
MINCED CHICKEN IN LETTUCE CUPS

36
PORK AND SHRIMP GYOZA

39
SPICY SAKE PICKLES

40
SPAM MUSUBI

Tips for Grilling

Hawaiians are blessed with a climate perfect for outdoor cooking, but of course, this method of preparing food was around for centuries before a kettle grill was ever delivered to an Island hardware store. The imu is the pit used to cook the famous *kalua* pig. The Portuguese brought above-ground clay ovens to Hawaii. These were mainly used to bake bread, and some old ones can still be found scattered around Maui.

These days, cooks can choose between the traditional charcoal grill or a propane model. Let's not get into which one is "better," because they both have their advantages. No matter which one you prefer, the basic techniques apply to both.

DIRECT AND INDIRECT HEAT

DIRECT HEAT means that the food is cooked right over the heat source. This method is mainly used for ingredients that cook quickly, such as steaks, burgers, boneless chicken, and seafood. For a charcoal grill, build a charcoal fire and let it burn until the coals are covered with white ash. Dump the coals in the center of the grill. Do not spread the coals to the very edges of the grill, because you want a cooler area to move the food to if it drips and starts to flare up. For a gas grill, simply preheat the grill on high, then adjust the temperature as needed.

INDIRECT HEAT cooks food by radiant heat, with the food placed away from the source of heat to cook slowly. Large cuts of meat, including whole chicken and bone-in poultry parts, are best cooked by indirect heat. Often, wood is added to the grill to smolder and add a smoky flavor. In Hawaii, kiawe is the wood of choice for this purpose, and mesquite has a very similar flavor. For a charcoal grill, dump the coals on one side of the grill and leave the other side empty. Put an inexpensive aluminum foil pan on the empty side as a drip pan, and fill about halfway with water to help keep the heat distribution even. For a gas grill, preheat the grill on high, then turn one burner off. If there is room, put a foil pan under the cooking grate.

TWO-ZONE COOKING is a combination of the two methods. This works beautifully for cooking foods on skewers, as it allows the cook to protect the wooden skewers from burning. Set the fire up for indirect cooking. Line up the skewers on the grill with the meat directly over the fire, but keep the handles over the cooler area. Slip two long strips of aluminum foil under the skewers, with one strip under the handles and another under the exposed tips.

TEMPERATURE

The key to successful grilling is the correct temperature. If the heat is too high, the food burns; too low, and it lacks the caramelized surface that adds that special "sizzling" flavor. Remember that grilled food is meant to be cooked, not incinerated! Some grills come with thermometers built into their lids so you can check the temperature, which is a great feature. Otherwise, purchase a grill thermometer so you can keep track of the heat.

With a charcoal grill, the heat is controlled by vents on the top and bottom of the unit. Fire needs oxygen to stay alive. Open the vents wide, and the oxygen feeds the fire so it burns hot. Close them to cut off the oxygen, and the heat burns at a lower temperature. You can also let the coals burn down to reach the proper temperature. Whether your grill is charcoal or gas, always cook with the grill closed as much as possible to keep flare-ups to a minimum and contain the heat.

The heat ranges for grilling temperatures are:

HOT: 450°F/230°C to 550°F/290°C and above

MEDIUM: 350°F/180°C to 450°F/230°C

LOW: 300°F/150°C to 350°F/180°C

VERY LOW: 250°F/120°C to 300°F/150°C

The tiki era of entertaining, which blossomed after World War II, celebrated Island living with colorful tropical cocktails and Asian-inspired (if culturally inaccurate) food. It has triumphantly returned after a brief hiatus—although at Tommy Bahama, it never really went away. Crab rangoon, crispy wontons stuffed with seafood and cream cheese, is a fine example of the spirited genre.

CRAB RANGOON

PINEAPPLE MUSTARD

½ cup/155 g pineapple preserves

2 Tbsp Dijon mustard

CRAB RANGOON

4 oz/115 g cream cheese, at room temperature

2 tsp soy sauce

1 green onion, white and green parts, minced

1 garlic clove, minced

¼ tsp red pepper sauce

4 oz/115 g crabmeat (backfin is fine), picked over for cartilage

Cornstarch, for dusting

24 wonton squares (about half a 12-oz/340-g package)

1 large egg white, beaten with a pinch of salt until foamy, for sealing wontons

Vegetable oil, for deep-frying

1 To make the pineapple mustard: Stir the ingredients together in a small bowl to combine. Cover and let stand at room temperature until serving.

2 To make the crab rangoon: Mash the cream cheese, soy sauce, green onion, garlic, and red pepper sauce together in a medium bowl with a rubber spatula. Stir in the crabmeat.

3 Line a baking sheet with waxed paper and dust it with cornstarch. Place a wonton in front of you, with the points facing north, south, east, and west. Lightly brush the edges with egg white. Place 1 rounded tsp of the filling in the lower half of the wonton. Fold the north tip over to meet the south tip and press the open sides closed. Press the filling in the wonton to spread and flatten it slightly. Fold the east and west tips to meet in the center of the wonton and seal them together with a dab of egg white. Place on the baking sheet. Repeat with the remaining filling and wontons. Cover loosely with plastic wrap and refrigerate until ready to cook, up to 2 hours. Remove from the refrigerator about 30 minutes before cooking.

4 Position a rack in the center of the oven and preheat the oven to 200°F/95°C. Place a wire cake rack on a large rimmed baking sheet.

5 Pour 2 in/5 cm oil into a deep, heavy saucepan and heat over high heat to 350°F/180°C on a deep-frying thermometer. In batches without crowding, add the wontons and deep-fry, turning them as needed, until golden brown, about 2 minutes. Using a wire spider or a slotted spoon, transfer the wontons to the wire rack and keep warm in the oven while frying the remaining wontons.

6 Transfer to a serving platter and serve warm, with the pineapple mustard.

MAKES 6 TO 8 SERVINGS

Although it says "Hawaiian vacation" as definitively as surfboards and ukuleles, coconut shrimp is probably another invention from one of the originators of the tiki craze, Donn Beach or "Trader" Vic Bergeron. Here is our version, served from Tokyo to Florida. Depending on the occasion, you can serve the shrimp plated with Asian slaw as a first course, or heaped on a platter with the sauce as a dip.

TOMMY'S FAMOUS COCONUT SHRIMP

SAUCE

One 9-oz/255-g jar Major Grey's mango chutney

1 Tbsp Dijon mustard

1 Tbsp mango nectar or pineapple juice

BATTER

¾ cup/105 g dry seafood fry mix or unbleached all-purpose flour

1 cup/240 ml lager beer

5 large egg yolks

4 tsp sugar

1¼ tsp kosher salt

½ tsp freshly ground black pepper

Vegetable oil, for deep-frying

½ cup/70 g unbleached all-purpose flour

¾ cup/60 g sweetened coconut flakes

16 extra-jumbo (16 to 20 count) shrimp, peeled and deveined, tail segment left intact

½ recipe Asian Slaw (page 58), for serving (optional)

1 **To make the sauce:** Purée the ingredients in a blender. Transfer to a small bowl, cover, and set aside until serving.

2 **To make the batter:** Whisk the ingredients together in a large bowl. Let stand for 10 to 15 minutes.

3 Position a rack in the center of the oven and preheat the oven to 200°F/95°C. Pour 2 in/5 cm oil into a large, deep saucepan and heat over high heat to 350°F/180°C.

4 Spread the flour in a shallow bowl. Spread the coconut in a second bowl. Place a wire rack on a large rimmed baking sheet. One at a time, toss the shrimp in the flour, then in the batter, letting the excess batter drip back into the bowl. Roll the shrimp in the coconut to coat evenly. Transfer to a platter.

5 In batches, without crowding, deep-fry the shrimp, turning them halfway through frying, until golden brown, about 2½ minutes. Using a wire spider or a slotted spoon, transfer the shrimp to the wire rack and keep warm in the oven while frying the rest.

6 To serve as a first course, for each serving, spoon one-quarter of the slaw in the center of a salad plate. Spread a scant 1 Tbsp sauce at the 12-o'clock position of the plate, then 1 Tbsp each at 3, 6, and 9 o'clock. Top each serving of sauce with a shrimp and serve. To serve informally, pour the sauce into a small serving bowl, heap the shrimp on a platter, and serve with the sauce as a dip.

MAKES 4 SERVINGS

Poke (PO-kay), or marinated chopped seafood (*poke* means "to cut"), is the Island version of ceviche and an essential luau dish. Layered with guacamole, poke has become one of our restaurants' signature recipes as a plated first course to serve with flatbread. We use a metal ring mold to give the stack a tailored look, or you can have a hardware store cut 3-in/7.5-cm PVC pipe to the right depth.

TUNA POKE WITH GUACAMOLE AND FLATBREAD

TUNA POKE

2½ Tbsp Asian sesame oil

2½ Tbsp soy sauce

1½ Tbsp fresh lime juice

1½ Tbsp minced shallots

1½ tsp peeled and minced fresh ginger

1½ tsp adobo from canned chipotles in adobo

18 oz/570 g fresh sushi-grade tuna, cut into ⅓-in/8-mm dice

2 Tbsp rinsed nonpareil capers

2 Tbsp finely chopped fresh cilantro

GUACAMOLE

1½ large ripe avocados, peeled and pitted (reserve ½ avocado for the Avocado Wasabi Cream)

2 large, ripe Roma tomatoes, about 11 oz/310 g, seeded and cut into ¼-in/6-mm dice

1 green onion, white and green parts, finely chopped

1 Tbsp fresh lime juice

1 Tbsp finely chopped fresh cilantro

1 Tbsp finely chopped shallot

⅛ tsp cayenne pepper

½ tsp kosher salt

AVOCADO WASABI CREAM

½ ripe avocado, peeled and pitted (see preceding list)

2 tsp fresh lime juice

1 tsp wasabi powder

Pinch of sugar

1 Tbsp sour cream

Kosher salt

Fresh cilantro sprigs, for serving

Flatbread, for serving

SPECIAL EQUIPMENT: One stainless steel entremet ring (also called a round mold), 3 in/7.5 cm in diameter and 1½ in/4 cm tall, available at restaurant suppliers and online; pastry bag with ½-in/12-mm open star tip.

1 **To make the poke:** Whisk the sesame oil, soy sauce, lime juice, shallots, ginger, and chipotle adobo together in a medium bowl. Add the tuna, capers, and cilantro and mix well.

2 **To make the guacamole:** Mix all the ingredients (except the reserved ½ avocado) together in a medium bowl. Press plastic wrap onto the guacamole surface. Cover and refrigerate the poke and guacamole until chilled, at least 1 hour or up to 1 day.

3 **To make the wasabi cream:** Using a fork, thoroughly mash the ½ avocado in a small bowl until it is as smooth as possible; you should have a heaping ⅓ cup/70 g. Mix the lime juice, wasabi, and sugar together in a ramekin and stir into the avocado with the sour cream. Season to taste with the salt. Cover and refrigerate until chilled, at least 1 hour or up to 1 day.

4 Transfer the wasabi cream to a pastry bag fitted with a ½-in/12-mm open star tip. Have ready a ring mold 3 in/7.5 cm in diameter and 1½ in/4 cm tall. For each serving, place the mold in the center of a dinner plate. Spread one-sixth (about 100 g) of the guacamole in the mold, and top with one-sixth (about 100 g) of the poke. Lift up and remove the mold. Pipe a rosette of the wasabi cream on top of the tuna. Garnish with the cilantro sprigs. Serve immediately, with the flatbread.

MAKES 6 SERVINGS

This could be the ultimate bar food. From Hong Kong to Honolulu and beyond, fried shrimp is universally loved. In this case, the sweet little crustaceans are coated with a spicy sauce that is even better when the heat is doused with quantities of an icy beverage. Serve these on small plates, or plan on doing a lot of finger licking.

CRISPY SRIRACHA SHRIMP

SAUCE

½ cup/120 ml mayonnaise

2 tsp Sriracha or chili garlic sauce

SHRIMP

⅔ cup/90 g unbleached all-purpose flour

⅔ cup/80 g cornstarch

1 tsp kosher salt

½ tsp freshly ground black pepper

1 cup/240 ml buttermilk

1½ lb/680 g large (31 to 35 count) shrimp, peeled and deveined

Vegetable oil, for deep-frying

Lime wedges, for serving

1 **To make the sauce:** Whisk the ingredients together in a small bowl. Cover and set aside for 20 to 30 minutes.

2 **To make the shrimp:** Whisk the flour, cornstarch, salt, and pepper together in a large bowl. Pour the buttermilk into a second large bowl and add the shrimp. A few at a time, lift the shrimp from the buttermilk and toss in the flour mixture to coat. Transfer to a baking sheet or platter and let stand to set the coating while the oil is heating.

3 Preheat the oven to 200°F/95°C. Pour 2 in/5 cm oil into a large, heavy saucepan and heat over high heat to 350°F/180°C on a deep-frying thermometer. Place a wire rack on a rimmed baking sheet. In batches, without crowding, add the shrimp to the hot oil and deep-fry until crisp and golden brown, about 2½ minutes. Using a wire spider or slotted spoon, transfer to the wire rack to drain, and keep warm in the oven while deep-frying the remaining shrimp.

4 Transfer the fried shrimp to a large bowl. Add the sauce and toss well. Divide equally among small plates and serve immediately, with the lime wedges.

MAKES 4 TO 6 SERVINGS

Like poke, lomi-lomi salmon is a luau dish that can also be served as an appetizer with flatbread as a Hawaiian "bruschetta." The Islanders learned how to salt salmon from Westerners, and combined it with fresh ingredients for this cross between a salad and a salsa that is mixed to blend the flavors (lomi means "massage"). Lox is a great substitute for salted salmon.

LOMI-LOMI SALMON WITH TOMATOES AND ONIONS

8 oz/225 g lox, cut into ½-in/12-mm dice

1 large beefsteak tomato, seeded and cut into ½-in/12-mm dice

½ cup/75 g diced sweet onion, preferably Maui

2 green onions, white and pale green parts, finely chopped

Flatbread, for serving

1 Refrigerate the lox in a bowl of ice water to cover until some of the salt flavor is removed, 1 to 2 hours. Drain well.

2 Mix the drained lox, tomato, onion, and green onions (preferably with your fingertips, the better to release some of the tomato juices) in a medium bowl. The lomi-lomi should be served ice-cold, so mix in a few ice cubes. Serve chilled with the flatbread.

MAKES 8 SERVINGS

Tips for Mixing and Serving Cocktails

The recipe for a great party is equal parts high-quality food, friends, and beverages, well shaken. These days, bars have upped the ante on cocktails, offering a huge range of drinks, from the historical (including those from the newly revived tiki era, which in our world, never went away) to the cutting-edge. A good party-giver has to know how to make more than a gin and tonic. Handing your guest a Mai Tai definitely makes a statement.

EQUIPMENT CHECKLIST

You will need a few bartending tools to make top-notch cocktails:

BOSTON COCKTAIL SHAKER: Preferred by professional bartenders, this two-part shaker has a glass bottom and a metal top of about the same size. Using it is fairly self-explanatory: Fill the bottom half with ice, add the cocktail ingredients, cover tightly with the metal top, and shake briskly a few times (most bartenders say for 10 seconds) to mix the ingredients. (Of course, some drinks should be stirred, not shaken—where have you heard that before? Shaking creates foam, and who wants a foamy martini?) Boston shakers are used in conjunction with a cocktail strainer to get the drink out of the glass. A shaker with a strainer built into the lid is called a cobbler shaker, and they work well, too.

COCKTAIL STRAINER: A strainer is placed over the glass bottom of a shaker to hold back the ice for pouring. There are two kinds, and they work equally well. The Hawthorne strainer has a spring running around its perimeter so it fits snugly in the shaker. The julep strainer is simply a perforated metal lid, slightly curved to fit into the shaker. In either case, the strainer is held in place at the top of the shaker with your first two fingers as you wrap the rest of your hand around the shaker to hold it for pouring.

COCKTAIL SPOON: A long-handled spoon that can reach all the way into the bottom of a shaker to efficiently stir a drink. An iced-tea spoon will work.

MUDDLER: Use this pestle to mash up fruit and other ingredients in the shaker so they can release their juices into the drink. You'll find metal, plastic, and wood models.

JIGGER: In America, a jigger is a measurement of 1½ fl oz/45 ml, but it is also the name of the small measuring glass with the same volume. Cocktail ingredients need to be measured, just like any other ingredients. Jiggers come in a variety of sizes and designs, and can be unmarked, so be sure that you know the exact volume of the one on your bar. If you are making your cocktails in a country that uses another measuring system, such as British or metric, use your locality's jigger, which may be slightly larger than the U.S. one. Cocktails are also mixed according to increments, so for conversion purposes, it is easy to go by "parts" instead of ounces. For example, 1 fl oz/30 ml liquor with ½ fl oz/15 ml fruit juice can be translated as 1 part and ½ part. This way, you won't have to measure 7.5 ml to equal ¼ fl oz.

KEEP IT FRESH

Many cocktails get their lip-smacking flavor from the proper balance of liquor with a sweet and sour component, and fresh fruit juices are an important part of the equation. Too many bars lean on instant sour mixes—you can do better. We make our own sour mix from scratch with sweetened fresh juices (page 167). Fresh juices and other ingredients are also used to make tasty syrups for flavoring cocktails. These are usually based on simple syrup, which is no more than equal parts superfine sugar and water shaken together to dissolve the sugar.

Be sure you have an efficient juicer. A wooden reamer is good, but if you are juicing a lot of fruit, consider a metal lever-type squeezer or even an inexpensive electric model.

GARNISHES

Garnishes don't exactly make the drink, but they do add an extra dose of festivity to the glass. Maraschino cherries have been garnishing drinks for eons, but the American kind are artificially colored and most bartenders prefer not to use them these days. Imported Marasca cherries preserved in syrup (Luxardo is a reliable brand) can be found at well-stocked liquor stores and are worth the expense. As far as other garnishes are concerned, we don't have to tell you that we prefer chunks of fresh fruit to paper umbrellas.

In the late 1950s, the Hilton Hawaiian Village in Honolulu was asked to come up with a cocktail to show off blue curaçao, a new product at the time. Here's what bartender Harry Yee created, named for the song made famous by Bing Crosby (and subsequently a huge bestseller for Elvis Presley). Thanks to the yellow pineapple juice, be prepared for your drink to be closer in color to the blue of a cloudy sky and not that of the Pacific Ocean.

BLUE HAWAII

3 fl oz/90 ml pineapple juice

1 fl oz /30 ml From-Scratch Sour Mix (page 167)

¾ fl oz/22.5 ml white or silver rum

¾ fl oz/22.5 ml vodka

½ fl oz/15 ml blue curaçao

GARNISH: **Pineapple wedge, Marasca cherry**

1 Add the ingredients to an ice-filled cocktail shaker. Shake well.

2 Fill a tall Collins glass with ice. Strain the cocktail into the glass. Garnish with the pineapple and cherry and serve.

MAKES 1 DRINK

Don't wait until cherry blossoms are in bloom to enjoy this martini. In addition to cherry vodka, it has maraschino, a cherry liqueur that has very little to do with the artificially colored cherries of the same name. Luxardo is an Italian company that makes both the liqueur and the preserved Marasca cherries that are the preferred garnish of discerning bartenders. Delicious doesn't begin to describe this drink.

CHERRY BLOSSOM MARTINI

SIMPLE SYRUP

½ cup/100 g superfine sugar

COCKTAIL

2 fl oz/60 ml black cherry vodka, preferably Grey Goose Cherry Noir

1 fl oz/30 ml fresh lime juice

¾ fl oz/22.5 ml maraschino liqueur, preferably Luxardo

¾ fl oz/22.5 ml Simple Syrup, above

GARNISH: **2 Marasca cherries on a cocktail skewer**

1 **To make the simple syrup:** Shake the sugar and ½ cup/120 ml water together in a covered jar until the sugar is dissolved. (The syrup can be refrigerated for up to 1 month.)

2 Fill a martini glass with ice cubes and set aside to chill. Add the cocktail ingredients to an ice-filled cocktail shaker. Shake well.

3 Empty the ice from the glass. Strain the cocktail into the glass. Garnish with the skewer and serve.

MAKES 1 DRINK

Pupus, the little (and not-so-little) bites that Hawaiians serve to start the meal, are more than an appetizer. Dished up in large quantities, they can actually *be* the meal. Here's an example of a contemporary pupu: Korean-style chicken wings slathered in a thick sweet and hot sauce. While they are really no more fiery than Buffalo wings, it might be a good idea to offer ice cold beer alongside.

ROASTED KOREAN CHICKEN WINGS

MARINADE

¼ cup/60 ml soy sauce

2 Tbsp honey

2 Tbsp Chinese rice wine or dry sherry

2 green onions, white and green parts, minced

1 Tbsp peeled and minced fresh ginger

2 garlic cloves, minced

4 lb/1.8 kg chicken wings, cut between the joints, wing tips trimmed (see Note)

SAUCE

⅓ cup/100 g gochujang (Korean chili paste)

3 Tbsp soy sauce

2 Tbsp unseasoned rice vinegar

2 Tbsp honey

1 Tbsp Asian sesame oil

1 Tbsp peeled and minced fresh ginger

4 garlic cloves, minced

Sesame seeds, for garnish

1 To make the marinade: Whisk the ingredients together with 2 Tbsp water in a large bowl. Add the chicken wings and stir to coat them. Cover with plastic wrap and refrigerate for 2 to 4 hours.

2 Position a rack in the center of the oven and preheat the oven to 425°F/220°C. Line a large rimmed baking sheet with aluminum foil and lightly oil the foil.

3 Remove the chicken wings from the marinade, discarding the marinade. Arrange the wings on the prepared baking sheet. Roast for 20 minutes. Flip the wings over, and continue roasting until the wings are well browned and tender, about 25 minutes more.

4 Meanwhile, whisk the ingredients for the sauce together in a large bowl. Set aside while the chicken is roasting to blend the flavors.

5 Using tongs, transfer the chicken wings to the sauce in the bowl. Mix the wings well to coat them. Transfer to a platter. Sprinkle with the sesame seeds and serve with plenty of napkins.

MAKES 4 TO 6 SERVINGS

NOTE: Cut-up chicken wings (labeled drumettes or wingettes) tend to be frozen and give off a lot of liquid during roasting that discourages browning. For the best results, buy whole wings and cut them up at home, discarding the wing tips or saving them for another use (such as making a small batch of chicken stock).

Sweet onions—which lack the sulfur that makes your nose sting and your eyes tear—used to be quite exotic, but now you'll find one variety or another at your supermarket. Vidalia from Georgia, Walla Walla from Washington, or Texas Sweets are common, but Hawaiians naturally feel that the best ones come from the fertile slopes of Mount Haleakala. This indulgent dip is addictive and should come with a warning label. Of course, it is outstanding with potato chips, but try it as a dip for raw vegetables, too.

MAUI SWEET ONION, BACON, AND CHIVE DIP

3 slices bacon

1 Tbsp vegetable oil

2 sweet onions, preferably Maui, about 12 oz/340 g total, cut into ¼-in/6-mm dice

Kosher salt and freshly ground black pepper

1 cup/240 ml sour cream

2 Tbsp finely chopped fresh chives, plus more for garnish

1 tsp granulated onion

Potato chips or assorted raw vegetables, for serving

1 Cook the bacon in a medium nonstick skillet over medium heat, turning it occasionally, until crisp and browned, about 8 minutes. Transfer to paper towels to drain and cool. Discard the fat and wipe out the skillet with paper towels.

2 Add the oil to the skillet and heat over medium heat. Add the onions and sprinkle with ½ tsp salt and ¼ tsp pepper. Cover and cook, stirring occasionally, until the onions soften, about 5 minutes. Uncover and reduce the heat to medium-low. Cook, stirring occasionally, until the onions are deep golden brown, about 25 minutes. Transfer the onions to a medium bowl and let cool completely.

3 Finely crumble the bacon and add to the onions. Stir in the sour cream, the 2 Tbsp chives, and the granulated onion and season to taste with salt and pepper. Cover and refrigerate to blend the flavors, at least 1 hour or up to 2 days.

4 Transfer to a serving bowl. Sprinkle with chives to garnish and serve chilled, with the potato chips for dipping.

MAKES 6 TO 8 SERVINGS (2 CUPS/430 G)

The influence of Asian (and by association, Hawaiian) cuisine on mainstream American cooking is evident in these skewers. Once considered exotic, such ingredients as curry paste, coconut milk, and fish sauce are now sold at most supermarkets. To keep the wooden skewers from burning up over the fire, slip aluminum foil under the ends. The simple peanut sauce can also be used as a dip for potato chips or crudités.

PORK SATAY WITH PEANUT SAUCE

MARINADE

¾ cup/180 ml coconut milk (not cream of coconut)

3 Tbsp finely chopped shallots

2 Tbsp Thai or Vietnamese fish sauce

2 tsp peeled and minced fresh ginger

2 tsp light brown sugar

1½ tsp Thai yellow or red curry paste or Madras curry powder

2 garlic cloves, minced

2¼ lb/1.1 kg center-cut boneless pork loin, cut across the grain into 24 slices

PEANUT SAUCE

½ cup/155 g smooth peanut butter

⅓ cup/75 ml chicken stock or canned reduced-sodium chicken broth

2 Tbsp Thai or Vietnamese fish sauce

2 Tbsp unseasoned rice vinegar

2 Tbsp light brown sugar

1 Tbsp Thai yellow or red curry paste or Madras curry powder

1 Tbsp peeled and minced fresh ginger

2 garlic cloves, minced

24 bamboo skewers, soaked in water for 30 minutes and drained

1 To make the marinade: Whisk the ingredients together in a medium bowl. Add the pork slices and mix well to coat the pork. Cover with plastic wrap and refrigerate for at least 2 or up to 8 hours.

2 To make the sauce: Whisk the ingredients together with 2 Tbsp water in a medium bowl. Cover and refrigerate until ready to serve. (The sauce can be made up to 2 days ahead.)

3 Prepare an outdoor grill for two-zone cooking over medium heat (see page 19).

4 Thread the pork onto the skewers. Scrub the grill grate clean. Place the skewers with the meat directly over the heat source and the handles over the unlighted area. To protect the skewers from burning (even though they have been soaked), slip a long strip of foil underneath the handles and another strip underneath the exposed pointed tips. Cover and grill, turning occasionally, until the pork is opaque and cooked through, 12 to 15 minutes. Remove the skewers from the grill.

5 Pour the sauce into individual ramekins for dipping. Serve the skewers with the sauce.

MAKES 4 TO 6 SERVINGS

This Chinese recipe is usually prepared with boned squab meat, but you can substitute chicken thighs for a similar flavor. As with all stir-fries, it is important to have the ingredients prepared before you start cooking so the operation will go like clockwork. If you choose to use a food processor for chopping, be careful not to overprocess the ingredients into mush.

MINCED CHICKEN IN LETTUCE CUPS

6 dried shiitake mushrooms

CHICKEN AND MARINADE

1 lb/455 g skinless, boneless chicken thighs, frozen until partially firm, about 1 hour

1 Tbsp soy sauce

1 Tbsp oyster sauce

1 Tbsp Chinese rice wine or dry sherry

1 Tbsp cornstarch

½ cup/120 ml canned reduced-sodium chicken broth

1 tsp hoisin sauce, plus more for serving

¼ tsp red pepper flakes

2 Tbsp vegetable oil

One 8-oz/225-g can sliced water chestnuts, rinsed, drained, and cut into ¼-in/6-mm dice

1 small carrot, peeled and cut into ¼-in/6-mm dice

4 green onions, white and pale green parts, finely chopped

1 garlic clove, minced

12 iceberg lettuce leaves, for serving

1 Soak the dried mushrooms in boiling water to cover in a small bowl until the mushrooms are softened, 20 to 30 minutes.

2 Meanwhile, marinate the chicken: Using a large knife, cut the chicken thighs into 1-in/2.5-cm chunks and pulse in a food processor until coarsely minced. Transfer the minced chicken to a medium bowl. Add the soy sauce, oyster sauce, rice wine, and cornstarch and mix well. Let stand at room temperature for about 20 minutes.

3 Drain the mushrooms; cut off and discard the stems. Cut the mushroom caps into ¼-in/6-mm dice. Stir the broth, the 1 tsp hoisin, and the red pepper flakes together in a small bowl.

4 Heat a large wok or skillet over medium-high heat. Add the oil and heat until very hot and shimmering. Add the chicken and its marinade and cook, stirring often, until the chicken is opaque. Add the diced mushrooms, water chestnuts, carrot, green onions, and garlic and cook, stirring often, until the vegetables are hot, about 1 minute. Stir in the broth mixture and cook until it has reduced to a glaze and coats the chicken mixture, about 1 minute.

5 Transfer the chicken mixture to a medium bowl. Place the lettuce leaves on a platter. Serve the chicken mixture and lettuce with a bowl of hoisin sauce for seasoning. Let each guest fill a lettuce cup with the chicken mixture, add a dab of hoisin (if desired), and roll up the lettuce to eat.

MAKES 4 TO 6 SERVINGS

Gyoza, the Japanese version of pot stickers, are fried in a skillet until one side is browned, forming a crisp counterpoint to the rest of the tender shell and its juicy filling. It's nice to have some help folding the gyoza, so enlist a friend to jump in. You could even enlist your guests as party helpers. Serve the piping hot gyoza as a plated first course, or binge on them as a lunch or supper dish.

PORK AND SHRIMP GYOZA

DIPPING SAUCE

½ cup/120 ml soy sauce

¼ cup/60 ml unseasoned rice vinegar

1 green onion, white and green parts, thinly sliced

FILLING

8 oz/225 g large (31 to 35 count) shrimp, peeled, deveined, and tails removed

8 oz/225 g ground pork

2 green onions, white and green parts, minced

2 garlic cloves, minced

1 Tbsp soy sauce

1 tsp Chinese rice wine or dry sherry

1 tsp Asian sesame oil

¼ tsp kosher salt

⅛ tsp freshly ground black pepper

1 package round gyoza wrappers (about 5 dozen)

2 Tbsp vegetable oil, plus more as needed

1 To make the dipping sauce: Mix the ingredients together in a medium bowl.

2 To make the filling: Pulse the shrimp in a food processor until ground into a coarse paste. (Or chop finely with a large knife.) Transfer to a medium bowl. Add the ground pork, green onions, garlic, soy sauce, rice wine, sesame oil, salt, and pepper and mix well.

3 Line a large baking sheet with waxed or parchment paper. For each dumpling, place 1 tsp of the filling on the bottom half of a dumpling wrapper. Moisten the edges of the wrapper with water. Fold the wrapper in half to enclose the filling and press the open edges closed. Starting at the center of curve, pleat the top of the gyoza with six or seven small, tight folds. Stand the gyoza, pleated side up, on the baking sheet.

4 Heat the 2 Tbsp oil in a very large nonstick skillet over medium-high heat until hot and shimmering. In batches, stand the gyoza in the skillet, pleated side up. Cook until the bottoms are golden brown, about 1 minute. Carefully pour in about 1 cup/240 ml water (it will boil up) and tightly cover. Boil for 3 minutes. Uncover and cook until the water has evaporated and the gyoza are sizzling, about 3 minutes more. (Or use two skillets to speed the cooking along.) Transfer to a heat-proof serving platter and keep the gyoza warm in a preheated 200°F/95°C oven, loosely covered with aluminum foil, while cooking the remainder. Wipe out the skillet with paper towels between batches, and add more oil as needed to cook the gyoza.

5 Pour the dipping sauce into ramekins. Serve the gyoza with the sauce.

MAKES ABOUT 5 DOZEN DUMPLINGS

BLOOMFIELD
200
INDUSTRIES
U.S.A.

It's cocktail time, and you could use a little something to nibble on to accompany the beverage of your choice. In just a few minutes, you can turn raw vegetables into tangy Asian-style pickles. Feel free to experiment with other vegetables, such as red bell pepper, cauliflower, celery, or daikon. Cut into strips, sticks, or slices about ¼ in/6 mm wide to allow the pickling liquid to penetrate them quickly.

SPICY SAKE PICKLES

3 unpeeled Persian or Kirby cucumbers, or ½ English (seedless) cucumber, scrubbed

2 carrots, peeled

3 Tbsp unseasoned rice vinegar

3 Tbsp good-quality sake, such as Gekkeikan Traditional

1 Tbsp soy sauce

2 tsp honey, or 1 tsp light brown sugar

½ tsp hot red pepper sauce, such as Sriracha

One 1-in/2.5-cm piece fresh ginger, peeled and cut into thin sticks

Asian sesame oil, for serving

Sesame seeds, for garnish

1 Cut the cucumbers and carrots lengthwise into strips about ¼ in/6 mm wide and 3 in/7.5 cm long.

2 Whisk the vinegar, sake, soy sauce, honey, and hot pepper sauce together in a shallow glass or ceramic dish. Add the ginger and crush it a bit with a spoon. Add the cucumbers and carrots and toss to coat. Refrigerate for at least 15 minutes or up to 2 hours.

3 Transfer the vegetable mixture with some of the pickling juices to a serving dish. Drizzle with the sesame oil, sprinkle with the sesame seeds, and serve.

MAKES 4 TO 6 SERVINGS

Basically, musubi is Spam sushi (although it's officially in the onigiri category, because the rice is not vinegared). This snack proudly celebrates Hawaii's affection for the canned meat (more than 5½ cans a year per person!), which started in the years after World War II and continues unabated. Don't bother to buy a musubi mold, as these are easy to form by hand.

SPAM MUSUBI

2 cups/430 g medium-grain rice, such as Calrose

One 12-oz/340-g can Spam, cut crosswise into 8 equal slices

2 Tbsp soy sauce

2 Tbsp sake or dry sherry

2 Tbsp light brown sugar

About 3 Tbsp *furikake* (Japanese seaweed and sesame seasoning) or toasted sesame seeds

4 sheets toasted nori, cut in half to make 8 pieces

1 Rinse the rice in a sieve under cold running water. Put the rice in a medium saucepan and add 4 cups/960 ml cold water. (It is unnecessary to add salt to the cooking water because the musubi will be seasoned with the other ingredients, which are salty.) Bring to a boil over high heat. Reduce the heat to low and tightly cover the saucepan. Cook until the rice has absorbed the water, about 20 minutes. Remove from the heat and let stand, covered, for 10 minutes to let the rice settle. Uncover and let cool until the rice is warm but can be handled, about 10 minutes more.

2 Cook the Spam in a large nonstick skillet over medium-high heat, turning once, until lightly browned, 3 to 4 minutes. Transfer the Spam to a plate. Add the soy sauce, sake, brown sugar, and 2 Tbsp water to the skillet and bring to a boil, stirring to dissolve the sugar. Return the Spam to the skillet and cook, turning occasionally, until the liquid has reduced to a glaze and the Spam is caramelized, about 2 minutes. Return the Spam to the plate.

3 Place a bowl of water on the work surface. Using wet fingers, shape ⅓ cup/50 g of the rice into a rectangle on the work surface—it should be about ¾ in/2 cm thick and the length and width of a piece of Spam. Sprinkle ½ tsp of the *furikake* over the rice. Top with a slice of Spam and sprinkle with another ½ tsp of *furikake*. Top with ⅓ cup/50 g of rice and press the rice onto the Spam to make what resembles a Spam-and-rice sandwich.

4 Place a piece of nori on the work surface, the long side facing you and the shiny side facing down. Slip a long knife under the rice "sandwich" to loosen it, if necessary, and place it vertically in the center of the nori. Wrap the nori around the rice, sealing the edges with a dab of water. Using a sharp, thin knife, cut the musubi crosswise into 4 equal pieces. Transfer to a platter. Serve immediately. (The musubi can be covered and stored at room temperature for up to 2 hours, but they are best eaten before the nori softens.)

MAKES 32 PIECES

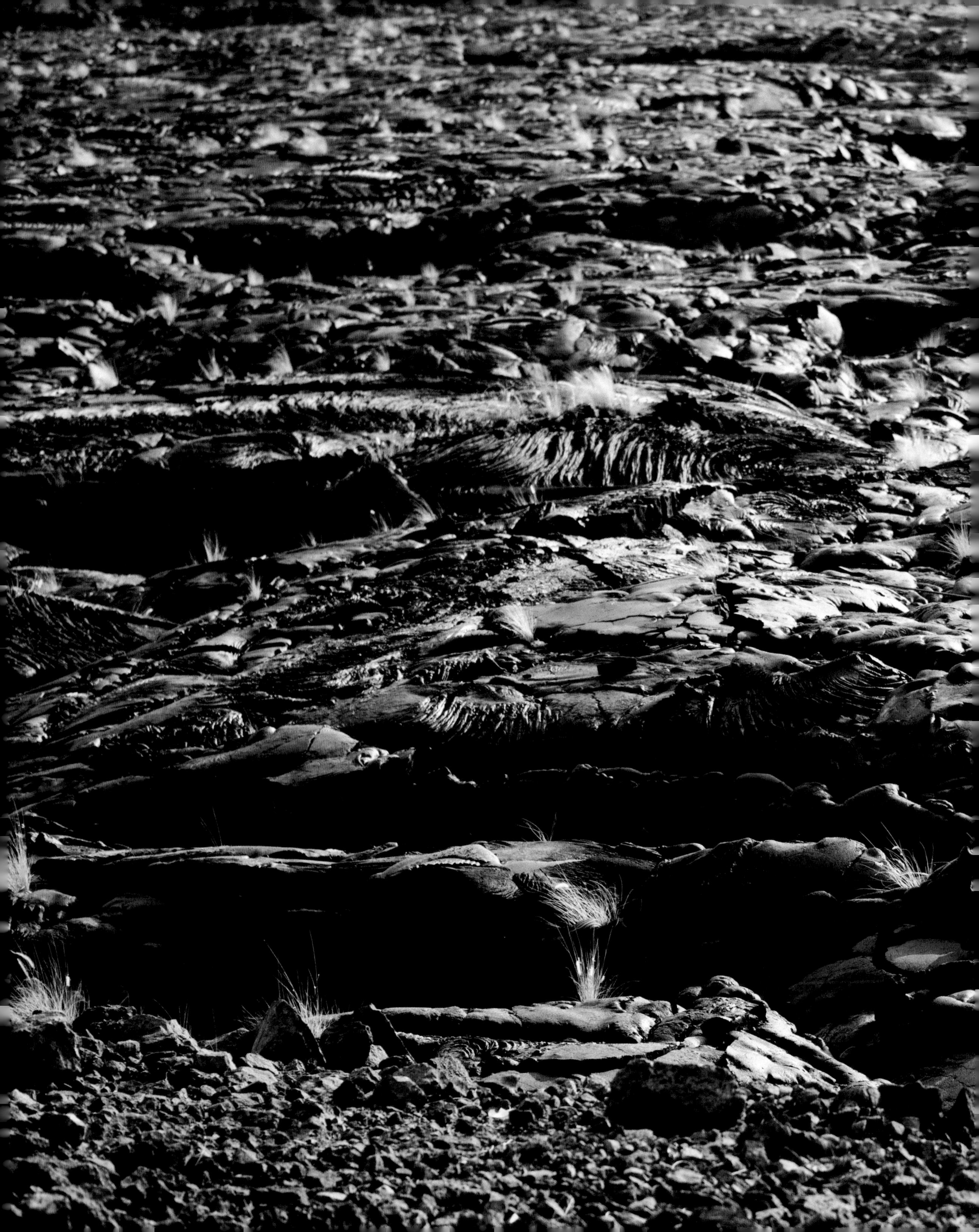

Of the four natural elements featured in this book, earth is, literally, the one on which we are grounded. Not only does it provide a platform for living, but it is also the soil from which all things grow. In Hawaiian mythology, Ku, the supreme god, was married to Hina, the Earth mother. But (as do mortals) the gods had a weakness for extramarital affairs, and Hina fell in love with Kane, god of the woods and all living creatures. Their love affair produced the first man.

Perhaps most noteworthy of all the Hawaiian deities was Lono, god of agriculture and fertility. His association with the Earth and renewal gave him a gentle nature connected with music and peace. From a Tommy Bahama perspective, Lono provides us with the ultimate lifestyle inspiration. Indeed, an afternoon snooze following a leisurely lunch may be the best way to honor the spirit of Lono. Alternatively, you can share a round of Blue Hawaiis (page 29) with friends and toast the good life!

The first Hawaiian settlers arrived some fifteen hundred years ago in outrigger canoes. They, too, were looking for the good life and brought along crops that have become Island staples, such as taro, sugarcane, bananas, coconuts, and breadfruit. Pineapples were not introduced to the Islands until 1817. Coffee arrived shortly afterward, and Hawaii remains the only state in the nation to grow coffee today.

By the 1800s, large ships and international commerce opened mainland markets to the vegetables, fruits, and nuts grown in Hawaiian soil. The demand for Hawaiian sugarcane, pineapples, and macadamia nuts skyrocketed. Today, however, modern-day farming has taken a more balanced, integrated approach to agriculture that would surely please the god Lono were he to return home for a visit. Sugarcane, pineapples, and macadamia nuts retain their place in the sun. But traditionally diverse crops such as taro, papaya, and Island flowers have regained importance, along with the many other garden vegetables and fruits at the core of every Tommy Bahama restaurant menu.

Our restaurants are blessed with the freshest ingredients from the breadbasket of the Pacific. And the creativity of our chefs, when paired with this Hawaiian bounty, is apparent in every recipe found in these pages.

EARTH

SOUPS AND SALADS

Even though Hawaii is warm most of the year, soups play a large part in its cuisine because they were an easy way for plantation cooks to feed hungry crews. And refreshing and colorful salads show off the array of Island produce in both classic and innovative ways.

45
ONO OXTAIL AND GREENS SOUP

46
CLAM SOUP WITH SHIITAKES AND MISO

48
RED BEAN AND HAM SOUP

50
MANDARIN HOT AND SOUR SOUP

51
TOM YUM SHRIMP SOUP

53
GREEN PAPAYA AND SHRIMP SALAD

54
ARUGULA, FRUIT, AND GOAT CHEESE SALAD WITH PAPAYA VINAIGRETTE

57
CITRUS AND HEARTS OF PALM SALAD WITH KUMQUAT VINAIGRETTE

58
ASIAN SLAW WITH GINGER DRESSING

59
ROMAINE HEARTS WITH MAUI ONIONS AND CARROT-MISO DRESSING

62
PLATE LUNCH POTATO-MACARONI SALAD

Ono is Hawaiian slang for "This is so good I could do the hula!" or something similar. You'll find this soup served at almost every lunch place on the Islands, and each version is a bit different from the next. Oxtails take forever to cook to tenderness, but when they finally melt down, the results rock. Go ahead and suck on the bones—everyone in Hawaii does.

ONO OXTAIL AND GREENS SOUP

4 Tbsp/60 ml vegetable oil, plus more as needed

3 lb/1.4 kg oxtails, cut crosswise into 2-in/5-cm pieces by butcher

1 large yellow onion, chopped

4 carrots, peeled and cut on the diagonal into 1-in/2.5-cm lengths

1 Tbsp peeled and minced fresh ginger

4 garlic cloves, minced

Zest of ½ orange, removed in strips with a vegetable peeler

2 star anise pods

4 oz/115 g unsalted roasted peanuts (1 cup)

12 oz/340 g Chinese greens such as bok choy or Chinese mustard, chopped into 1-in/2.5-cm pieces

2 Tbsp soy sauce, plus more for serving

Kosher salt and freshly ground black pepper

Chopped fresh cilantro, for garnish

1 Heat 2 Tbsp of the oil in a large soup kettle over medium-high heat. In batches, adding more oil as necessary, add the oxtails and cook, turning them occasionally, until browned, about 6 minutes. Transfer the oxtails to a plate.

2 Pour off the fat in the pot. Add the remaining 2 Tbsp oil and heat. Add the onion, carrots, ginger, and garlic and reduce the heat to medium. Cook, stirring occasionally, until softened, about 3 minutes. Return the oxtails to the pot and add cold water to cover them by 1 in/2.5 cm, about 8 cups/2 L. Bring to a boil over high heat, skimming off the foam that rises to the surface. Add the orange zest, star anise, and peanuts. Reduce the heat to medium-low and simmer, adding more water as needed to keep the oxtails covered, for 2½ hours. Add the greens and cook until both the greens and the oxtail meat are very tender, about 45 minutes more. (Remember, the soup will be eaten with a spoon, so the meat has to be falling off the bone.) Stir in the 2 Tbsp soy sauce and season to taste with salt and pepper. If you come across the orange peel and star anise, discard them.

3 Ladle the soup into deep bowls. Sprinkle with the cilantro and serve hot, with extra soy sauce passed on the side.

MAKES 8 SERVINGS

This Japanese-inspired soup, with its briny clam juices and the heady flavor of miso, is classy enough to serve at a dinner party, but easy to make in a smaller batch for a simple lunch. If you can, use beautiful Pacific (Manila) clams, although littlenecks are fine. Because miso and the clam juices will vary in saltiness, it is best to taste the broth to determine how much miso to add.

CLAM SOUP WITH SHIITAKES AND MISO

48 Manila or 36 littleneck clams

¼ cup/60 ml sake

1 garlic clove, minced

2 Tbsp white miso, plus more as needed

3 cups/720 ml boiling water

6 large shiitake mushrooms, stemmed, caps very thinly sliced

2 green onions, white and green parts, thinly sliced

1 Soak the clams in salted cold water for 1 hour. Drain and scrub well under cold running water.

2 Bring the sake and garlic to a boil in a large saucepan over high heat. Add the clams and cover. Cook until the clams open, about 5 minutes. Discard any unopened clams.

3 Using a wire spider or a slotted spoon, divide the clams equally among 6 soup bowls. If there is any sand or grit in the broth, strain it through a fine-mesh sieve, rinse the saucepan, and return the broth to the saucepan.

4 Add the 2 Tbsp miso to the boiling water in a saucepan and whisk to dissolve the miso. Stir the miso mixture into the saucepan and add the shiitakes. Bring just to a boil over high heat. Reduce the heat to low and simmer until the shiitakes are tender, about 2 minutes. Taste the soup; for a stronger flavor, whisk in more miso, 1 tsp at a time.

5 Ladle equal amounts of the soup into the bowls. Sprinkle with the green onions and serve immediately.

MAKES 6 SERVINGS

A Portuguese-Hawaiian staple, this sturdy soup will fill the kitchen with the appetizing aromas that promise good eating to come. It's the kind of food that was created to feed and fuel hungry people for a few more hours of labor in the sugar or pineapple factories. The soup does not use herbs, simply letting the ingredients mingle for a flavorful and satisfying dish to serve with crusty bread and green salad.

RED BEAN AND HAM SOUP

1 lb/455 g small red or red kidney beans, sorted over for stones, rinsed, and drained

2 ham hocks, about 1½ lb/680 g total

4 cups/960 ml canned reduced-sodium chicken broth

2 bay leaves

12 oz/340 g smoked sausage such as linguiça or chorizo, cut into ½-in/12-mm dice

1 small head green cabbage, about 2 lb/910 g, cored and chopped

1 large yellow onion, chopped

3 carrots, peeled and cut into ½-in/12-mm rounds

2 baking potatoes, peeled and cut into 1-in/2.5-cm cubes

3 garlic cloves, minced

Two 8-oz/225-g cans tomato sauce

Kosher salt and freshly ground black pepper

1 Put the beans in a large bowl and add cold water to cover by 1 in/2.5 cm. Let stand for at least 4 or up to 12 hours. If the weather is warm, refrigerate the beans in the bowl. (Or, put the beans in a large saucepan and add the water. Bring to a boil over high heat and cook for 2 minutes. Remove from the heat, cover tightly, and let stand for 1 hour.) Drain the beans.

2 Meanwhile, make a ham broth: Put the ham hocks, broth, and bay leaves in a stockpot and add 3 qt/2.8 L cold water. Bring to a boil over high heat. Reduce the heat to low and simmer uncovered for 1½ hours.

3 Put the beans in a large saucepan and add cold water to cover by 1 in/2.5 cm. Bring to a boil over high heat. Reduce the heat to medium-low and simmer until the beans are almost tender, 30 to 40 minutes. Drain the beans, reserving the cooking liquid.

4 Add the beans, sausage, cabbage, onion, carrots, potatoes, and garlic to the ham broth and pour in enough of the bean cooking liquid to cover the ingredients. Simmer until the ham hocks and vegetables are just tender, about 30 minutes. Transfer the ham hocks to a chopping board and let cool until easy to handle. Stir the tomato sauce into the soup and simmer for 5 to 10 minutes more. (Do not add the tomato sauce earlier, as it slows the cooking of the beans and potatoes.) Season to taste with salt and pepper. Discard the bay leaves.

5 Remove the meat from the ham hocks, discarding the skin and bones, and cut it into bite-size pieces. Stir into the soup and serve hot.

MAKES 8 TO 12 SERVINGS

Islanders love their soup and incorporate recipes from all over the world into their everyday cooking. Here is a classic Chinese soup loaded with dried flora such as tiger lily buds and tree ear mushrooms. Use the supermarket substitutions, and you will still have a great soup. (However, keep in mind that many of the Chinese ingredients will keep almost indefinitely for many future batches of soup.)

MANDARIN HOT AND SOUR SOUP

6 dried shiitake mushrooms

½ cup/15 g dried wood ear mushrooms, or one 8-oz/225-g can bamboo shoots, rinsed and drained

½ cup/30 g dried tiger lily buds, or one 8-oz/225-g can sliced water chestnuts, rinsed and drained

¼ cup/60 ml soy sauce

¼ cup/60 ml unseasoned rice vinegar

1 tsp chili sesame oil

¼ tsp freshly ground white pepper

3 Tbsp cornstarch

2 Tbsp vegetable oil

12 oz/340 g boneless pork loin chops or skinless, boneless chicken breast halves, cut across grain into pieces about ½ in/12 mm thick

5 cups/1.2 L Asian Chicken Broth (page 149) or canned reduced-sodium chicken broth

2 large eggs, beaten

6 oz/170 g firm tofu, cut into ½-in/12-mm cubes

2 green onions, white and green parts, chopped

1 In separate bowls, soak the shiitake mushrooms, wood ear mushrooms, and lily buds in hot water to cover until softened, 20 to 30 minutes. Drain each, but reserve 1 cup/240 ml of the shiitake soaking liquid. Cut off and discard the stems from the shiitake mushrooms and thinly cut the caps.

2 In a small bowl, mix the soy sauce, vinegar, chili sesame oil, and white pepper. Add the cornstarch and stir to dissolve. Set aside.

3 Heat the vegetable oil in a large, heavy saucepan over high heat. Add the pork strips and cook, stirring occasionally, until lightly browned, about 3 minutes. Transfer the pork to a plate.

4 Add the broth to the saucepan and bring to a boil. Stir the soy sauce mixture to blend in the cornstarch and stir into the broth. Return to a boil to thicken the soup. Stirring the soup, add the beaten eggs and cook until they form threads, about 1 minute. Return the pork and any juices to the saucepan and add the tofu and green onions. Remove from the heat and let stand for a few minutes to heat the tofu. Ladle into bowls and serve.

MAKES 6 SERVINGS

This is another Southeast Asian recipe with favorite Island flavors. These ingredients—including lemongrass, lime juice, ginger, and chiles—give depth and complexity to a soup that is really quite easy to make. Shrimp is the most common seafood used in this soup, but you can substitute thin rings of squid or chunks of snapper; cook them just until they turn opaque.

TOM YUM SHRIMP SOUP

2 Tbsp vegetable oil

⅓ cup/50 g chopped shallots

3 Tbsp peeled and minced lemongrass (tender bulb part only)

1 Tbsp peeled and minced fresh ginger

1 or 2 small fresh red chiles, minced with seeds

2 garlic cloves, minced

6 cups/1.4 L Asian Chicken Broth (page 149) or canned reduced-sodium chicken broth

¼ cup/60 ml fresh lime juice

¼ cup/60 ml Thai or Vietnamese fish sauce

1 Tbsp sugar

1 lb/455 g large (31 to 35 count) shrimp, peeled, deveined, and halved lengthwise

2 large ripe tomatoes, seeded and coarsely chopped

One 8-oz/225-g can sliced bamboo shoots, rinsed and drained

2 cups/150 g bean sprouts, for serving

2 Tbsp finely chopped fresh cilantro, for garnish

1 Heat the oil in a large saucepan over medium heat. Add the shallots, lemongrass, ginger, chiles, and garlic and cook until the shallots are softened, about 2 minutes. Add the broth, lime juice, fish sauce, and sugar and bring to a boil over high heat. Reduce the heat to low and simmer for 5 minutes.

2 Add the shrimp, tomatoes, and bamboo shoots. Cook just until the shrimp turn pink and opaque, about 2 minutes. Serve in soup bowls, topped with the bean sprouts and cilantro.

MAKES 6 SERVINGS

Papayas are a major Island crop for export, and the ones at your supermarket are likely to be the Hawaiian Solo variety. The fruits are shipped green, so your grocer may have unripened ones in storage. The dressing for this Southeast Asian salad is the perfect foil for the fruit's crisp, cucumber-like texture and relatively light flavor.

GREEN PAPAYA AND SHRIMP SALAD

DRESSING

Finely grated zest of 1 lime

¼ cup/60 ml fresh lime juice

3 Tbsp Thai or Vietnamese fish sauce

4 tsp sugar

½ tsp Sriracha sauce

1 unripe green papaya, about 1 lb/455 g, peeled, halved, and seeded

2 carrots, peeled

1 large tomato, seeded and cut into ½-in/12-mm dice

2 green onions, white and green parts, thinly sliced

½ cup/50 g chopped fresh cilantro

12 oz/340 g large (31 to 35 count) cooked, peeled, and deveined shrimp

3 Tbsp finely chopped unsalted dry-roasted peanuts

1 To make the dressing: Whisk the ingredients together in a small bowl.

2 Using a V-slicer, mandoline, or large knife, cut the papaya into julienne. Repeat with the carrots.

3 Mix the papaya, carrots, tomato, green onions, and cilantro with the dressing in a large bowl. Cover and refrigerate until chilled, at least 1 hour or up to 2 days.

4 Just before serving, stir in the shrimp. Using a slotted spoon, transfer the salad to individual plates. Sprinkle each serving with peanuts and serve chilled.

MAKES 6 SERVINGS

Fruit purée gives both body and flavor to salad dressings, and when the tropical fruit papaya is used, the results can be extraordinary. This vinaigrette includes the seeds, too, for a look and flavor similar to that of poppy seeds. The secret to this salad is the interplay of sweet fruit with tart cheese, crunchy walnuts, and peppery arugula. However, this dressing makes an event out of simple romaine or even iceberg lettuce.

ARUGULA, FRUIT, AND GOAT CHEESE SALAD WITH PAPAYA VINAIGRETTE

1 papaya, peeled

VINAIGRETTE

⅔ cup/110 g finely chopped papaya (above)

2 Tbsp papaya seeds (above)

2 Tbsp coarsely chopped shallots

½ cup/120 ml Asian sesame oil

⅓ cup/75 ml unseasoned rice vinegar

2 Tbsp raspberry or other fruit-flavored vinegar

1 Tbsp coarsely chopped fresh cilantro

Kosher salt and freshly ground black pepper

5 oz/140 g baby arugula

12 oz/340 g fresh strawberries, sliced

6 oz/170 g crumbled fresh white goat cheese (1 cup)

2 oz/60 g toasted and coarsely chopped walnuts (½ cup)

1 Using a spoon, scoop 2 Tbsp of the papaya seeds from the papaya and reserve them, discarding the remaining seeds. Cut the fruit into bite-size pieces. Finely chop and reserve ⅔ cup/110 g of the papaya. Transfer the remaining papaya to a bowl, cover, and refrigerate until ready to serve, up to 1 day.

2 To make the vinaigrette: Process the finely chopped papaya, papaya seeds, shallots, sesame oil, rice vinegar, raspberry vinegar, and cilantro together in a blender until the seeds are ground into tiny specks. Season to taste with salt and pepper. (The dressing can be transferred to a bowl, covered, and refrigerated for up to 1 day.)

3 To serve, toss the arugula in a large bowl with the vinaigrette. Divide the arugula mixture among 6 shallow bowls. Add equal amounts of the reserved papaya, the strawberries, and goat cheese to each salad, and sprinkle with the nuts. Serve immediately.

MAKES 6 SERVINGS

Summertime salads with tomatoes and basil are easy to love, but winter's bounty can make great salads, too. Kumquats originated in Asia, and are one of the many fruits that the Chinese brought to the Islands. Surprisingly, hearts of palm are new to the local culinary scene. If you happen to have fresh local hearts of palm, use less, as they are larger than the regular canned versions.

CITRUS AND HEARTS OF PALM SALAD WITH KUMQUAT VINAIGRETTE

DRESSING

¾ cup/180 ml olive oil (not extra-virgin)

6 kumquats, halved crosswise and seeded with the tip of a small, sharp knife

2 Tbsp fresh lemon juice, preferably from Meyer lemons

1½ tsp sugar

½ tsp kosher salt

A few grinds of black pepper

Leaves from 1 large head Bibb lettuce

6 drained hearts of palm, cut crosswise into ¼-in/6-mm rounds

2 navel oranges or grapefruits, peeled and cut between membranes into individual segments

1 shallot, thinly sliced

1½ tsp coarsely chopped fresh thyme

Kosher salt and freshly ground black pepper

1 **To make the dressing:** Purée the ingredients together in a blender. (The dressing can be transferred to a covered container and refrigerated for up to 2 days. Whisk it well before using.)

2 Toss the lettuce leaves, hearts of palm, orange segments, shallot, and thyme together in a large bowl. Add the dressing and toss gently. Season to taste with salt and pepper. Divide the salad among 4 salad plates and serve immediately.

MAKES 4 SERVINGS

This flavorful salad updates a beloved American standard with pan-Asian ingredients. Jícama, whose crisp texture holds up well in slaw, is often thought of as a Mexican tuber, but it is used in Vietnamese, Malaysian, and Chinese cuisines, too. If you can't find it, shredded carrots make a good substitute. The pineapple variation is especially tasty with *kalua* pork or ribs. The pineapple can also be broiled or pan grilled.

ASIAN SLAW WITH GINGER DRESSING

1 cup/240 ml mayonnaise

2 Tbsp unseasoned rice vinegar

2 Tbsp drained and chopped pickled ginger for sushi

1 tsp celery seeds

1 tsp sugar

½ green cabbage, shredded (about 6 cups/450 g)

½ jícama, peeled and julienned with a V-slicer or mandoline (about 2 cups/200 g)

½ red onion, cut into thin half-moons

¼ cup/25 g coarsely chopped fresh cilantro

Kosher salt and freshly ground white pepper

1 Whisk the mayonnaise, rice vinegar, ginger, celery seeds, and sugar together in a large bowl. Add the cabbage, jícama, red onion, and cilantro and mix well. Season to taste with salt and pepper. Cover and refrigerate until chilled, at least 2 hours or up to 2 days. Serve chilled.

MAKES 8 SERVINGS

GRILLED PINEAPPLE ASIAN SLAW: Cut 2 round slices of unpeeled pineapple, each about ¾ in/2 cm thick. Prepare an outdoor grill for direct cooking over high heat (see page 19). Lightly brush both sides of the pineapple with vegetable oil. Grill the pineapple, with the lid closed, turning once, until seared with grill marks on both sides, about 5 minutes. Transfer to a cutting board. Cut off the skin and remove the core. Coarsely chop the pineapple. Let cool and stir into the slaw.

The fresh colors and flavors in this salad are good enough for company, but you could toss it together for a weekend meal, too. You might recognize the salad from Japanese restaurants. The miso dressing is easily made in a blender. Because of its viscosity, it is especially good on sturdy, crisp lettuce such as romaine or iceberg.

ROMAINE HEARTS WITH MAUI ONIONS AND CARROT-MISO DRESSING

DRESSING

1 carrot, peeled and shredded on a box grater

1 green onion, white and pale green parts, coarsely chopped

2 Tbsp white miso

2 Tbsp Asian sesame oil

1 Tbsp peeled and coarsely chopped fresh ginger

2 tsp honey

1 garlic clove, coarsely chopped

Pinch of cayenne pepper

Leaves from 2 romaine hearts

1 cup/225 g small tomatoes, such as Toy Box or grape

½ small sweet onion, preferably Maui, cut into thin half-moons

2 Tbsp coarsely chopped fresh cilantro, for garnish

1 **To make the dressing:** Purée the ingredients in a blender with ⅓ cup/75 ml water.

2 Divide the lettuce leaves among 4 dinner plates, stacking the leaves on top of each other. Spoon equal amounts of the dressing over and around each lettuce stack. Scatter the tomatoes and onion around the lettuce and sprinkle with the cilantro. Serve immediately.

MAKES 4 SERVINGS

This concoction will keep vodka-lovers happy, not to mention pineapple fans. It starts with fresh pineapple, then gets a boost of fruit flavor from pineapple-flavored vodka. Because it is a guaranteed crowd pleaser, consider mixing up a big batch of this to serve in a pitcher or a punch bowl. To help the honey dissolve, mix the ingredients without ice, then add some cubes and shake it up.

PINEAPPLE PLANTATION

Three ¾-in/2-cm fresh pineapple chunks

¾ fl oz/22.5 ml fresh lemon juice

¾ fl oz/22.5 ml honey

2½ fl oz/75 ml pineapple-flavored vodka, preferably Van Gogh

GARNISH: **Pineapple wedge**

1 Fill a martini glass with ice cubes and set aside to chill. Muddle the pineapple with the lemon juice and honey in a cocktail shaker. Stir well without ice to dissolve the honey. Add ice and the vodka and shake well.

2 Empty the ice from the glass. Strain the cocktail into the chilled glass. Garnish with the pineapple and serve.

MAKES 1 DRINK

While some tropical drinks mix different kinds of rum, this refreshing beverage pairs two kinds of rum with bourbon. Passion fruit purée, available frozen at Latino markets, gives the drink a vibrant gold color. This is another drink that you might want to make in a big batch to serve as a punch.

TROPICAL ITCH

1½ fl oz/45 ml From-Scratch Sour Mix (page 167)

1½ fl oz/45 ml passion fruit purée

¾ fl oz/22.5 ml top-quality bourbon, such as Maker's Mark

¾ fl oz/22.5 ml aged gold or amber rum, preferably Cruzan Single Barrel

½ fl oz/15 ml overproof rum, such as Lemon Hart 151

½ fl oz/15 ml triple sec or Cointreau

2 dashes Angostura bitters

GARNISH: **Fresh mint sprig**

1 Add the ingredients to an ice-filled cocktail shaker. Shake well.

2 Fill a tall beer glass with ice. Strain the cocktail into the glass. Garnish with the mint and serve.

MAKES 1 DRINK

With a Hawaiian plate lunch, bigger is better. These inexpensive, filling meals always begin with a scoop or two of rice, paired with potato or macaroni salad. Because so many diners couldn't choose between the two salads, some inventive cook came up with this heavy-duty hybrid. It's great for backyard cookouts.

PLATE LUNCH POTATO-MACARONI SALAD

4 large unpeeled baking potatoes, scrubbed, about 1½ lb/680 g total

3 Tbsp unseasoned rice vinegar

8 oz/225 g short, tubular pasta such as ditalini or elbow macaroni

1¼ cups/300 ml mayonnaise, or more to taste

2 carrots, peeled and shredded

2 celery stalks, finely chopped

3 green onions, white and green parts, finely chopped

Kosher salt and freshly ground black pepper

1 Put the potatoes in a large saucepan and add salted cold water to cover by 1 in/2.5 cm. Cover and bring to a boil over high heat. Reduce the heat to medium and set the lid ajar. Cook at a brisk simmer until the potatoes are tender when pierced with the tip of a sharp knife, 20 to 30 minutes. Drain in a colander, rinse under cold running water, and let cool until easy to handle. Peel the potatoes and cut into bite-size pieces. Transfer to a bowl and sprinkle with the vinegar.

2 Meanwhile, bring a medium saucepan of water to a boil over high heat. Add the pasta and cook according to the package directions. Drain in a colander, rinse under cold running water, and add to the potatoes.

3 Add the mayonnaise, carrots, celery, and green onions to the potato mixture and mix well. Season to taste with salt and pepper. Cover and refrigerate until chilled, at least 2 hours or up to 1 day. Reseason with salt and pepper before serving cold.

MAKES 6 TO 8 SERVINGS

At age 63, Royce Hirayama is the oldest of his generation still working on his family's 30-acre produce farm in Kamuela. His love for growing things wore off on his son, Stennis, who grew up on the farm and is now Tommy Bahama's Executive Chef in Hawaii. Today Stennis lives on the farm in the same idyllic lifestyle embraced by his father, grandfather, and great grandfather, who immigrated to Hawaii from Japan. "It's a simple life," Chef Hirayama says. "People work hard, but they don't rush. They have a healthy attitude toward living."

At an early age, Hirayama began working in the fields planting seeds, boxing produce, and driving a tractor. This connection to the Earth and its edible produce inspired Stennis to pursue a formal culinary arts degree at Le Cordon Bleu in Oregon. After graduation, he honed his skills in mainland restaurants for 13 years until Tommy Bahama offered him the position of executive chef on the island of Hawaii.

"I always wanted to move back home," Hirayama says. His wife, who grew up on Maui, felt the same way. "We are very family oriented. There are 10 farmers living on our street, and we are all close—a bit like an extended family.

"We use both their produce and our produce in the restaurant," the chef continues. "It makes cooking very personal—not like buying from a wholesaler. Instead, everything is super fresh, grown by humble people who take great pride in their livelihood. My farm is only 20 minutes from the restaurant. I cut and bag our mixed greens literally minutes before going to work. You can't get much fresher than that!"

Chef Hirayama also takes advantage of many other edibles produced on the Islands, including macadamia nuts, coffee, tropical fruits like pineapples and coconuts, and—of course—sugarcane, which provides a natural, locally grown sweetener for many Island recipes. "There are cattle ranches here, too," Stennis says. "We support them as well."

Of course, the sea provides much inspiration for the chef's culinary palette. "There are so many fish in the waters here. We always get our fish fresh—never frozen," he says proudly. "The best thing about cooking in Hawaii is knowing where our food comes from. And at Tommy Bahama, we emphasize local ingredients produced on local farms by local people. It makes our restaurant more like our home."

HIRAYAMA FARMS, KAMUELA

POULTRY

Chickens were one of the first domesticated animals in the Islands, and there are countless feral flocks on Kauai and even Oahu. Hawaiians also have countless recipes for cooking the birds, using the various blends of international seasonings that make their cuisine unique.

67 GENERAL TSO'S CHICKEN

68 CHICKEN KATSU WITH UMAMI SAUCE

71 CHICKEN TERIYAKI WITH GRILLED SHIITAKE MUSHROOMS

72 CHICKEN YAKITORI

73 CHINESE ROAST DUCK WITH ORANGE-HONEY GLAZE

76 VIETNAMESE CHICKEN BREASTS WITH SAVORY CARAMEL SAUCE

79 CHICKEN AND BACON EMPANADAS

80 SWEET AND SOUR CHICKEN WITH MANGO AND ASPARAGUS

82 KUNG PAO CHICKEN

83 FRIED CHICKEN MOCHIKO

85 GRILLED CHICKEN BÁNH MÌ

Even though General Tso's chicken was invented in the United States by (some say) Taiwanese expats in New York City, this dish is as beloved in Hawaii as on the mainland. We include it here not because it is authentically Chinese, but because it is one of the best examples of Asian cooking, with exciting contrasts of crisp and tender, sweet and savory, spicy and sour in every bite.

GENERAL TSO'S CHICKEN

CHICKEN

1 lb/455 g boneless, skinless chicken thighs, cut into 1-in/2.5-cm pieces

2 large egg whites

1 Tbsp soy sauce

½ tsp freshly ground white pepper

SAUCE

½ cup/120 ml canned reduced-sodium chicken broth

1 Tbsp soy sauce

1 Tbsp tomato ketchup

1 Tbsp sugar

1 Tbsp unseasoned rice vinegar

1 tsp hoisin sauce

1½ tsp cornstarch

Vegetable oil

1 cup/125 g cornstarch

8 Chinese dried chiles

2 green onions, white and pale green parts, finely chopped

2 garlic cloves, minced

1 To marinate the chicken: Mix the ingredients in a medium bowl. Let stand for 10 to 20 minutes.

2 To make the sauce: Whisk the ingredients together in a small bowl.

3 Position a rack in the center of the oven and preheat the oven to 200°F/95°C. Place a wire rack on a large baking sheet. Heat a wok or large, deep saucepan over medium-high heat. Add 2 in/5 cm oil and heat to 350°F/180°C on a deep-frying thermometer.

4 Spread the cornstarch in a shallow dish. Working in batches and using a slotted spoon, remove the chicken from the marinade, letting the excess batter drip off, and roll the chicken in the cornstarch to coat. Transfer to a baking sheet and let stand for a few minutes to set the coating.

5 In batches without crowding, add the chicken to the oil and deep-fry until crisp and golden brown, about 3 minutes. Using a wire spider or a slotted spoon, transfer the chicken to the wire rack and keep warm in the oven while frying the rest. Carefully pour the oil out of the wok. Wipe out the wok with paper towels.

6 Heat the wok over medium-high heat. Add 2 Tbsp oil and heat the oil until it is very hot and shimmering. Add the chiles and stir just until darkened, about 10 seconds. (Chile fumes can be irritating, so don't breathe them in.) Add the green onions and garlic and stir until fragrant, about 10 seconds more. Quickly stirring the sauce mixture to blend, pour into the wok, and stir until it comes to a boil and thickens. Return the chicken to the wok and stir just until it is coated with the sauce, about 15 seconds. Transfer to a serving bowl and serve hot.

MAKES 4 SERVINGS

Panko quickly went from an ingredient you could only find at a Japanese market to a ubiquitous one. Chicken katsu is a panko-coated, fried cutlet that is even better when dipped in a homemade sauce. While you can buy bottled katsu sauce, this one is made with umami-rich ketchup and Worcestershire sauce, neither of which are very Asian but have been adopted by both Japanese and Hawaiian cooks.

CHICKEN KATSU WITH UMAMI SAUCE

UMAMI SAUCE

½ cup/120 g tomato ketchup

3 Tbsp Worcestershire sauce

2 Tbsp sugar

2 Tbsp mirin or sweet (amontillado) sherry

2 tsp peeled and minced fresh ginger

1 garlic clove, crushed through a press

4 skinless, boneless chicken breast halves, about 6 oz/170 g each

1 tsp kosher salt

½ tsp freshly ground black pepper

½ cup/70 g all-purpose flour

3 large eggs

1 cup/70 g panko (Japanese bread crumbs)

Vegetable oil, for frying

Lemon wedges, for serving

1 To make the sauce: Whisk the ingredients together in a medium bowl. Divide among 4 ramekins.

2 One at a time, place a chicken breast half between two plastic bags. Using the flat side of a meat pounder or a rolling pin, pound the chicken until about ½ in/12 mm thick. Season the chicken with the salt and pepper.

3 Spread the flour in a shallow bowl. Beat the eggs in a second shallow bowl. Spread the panko in a third. One at a time, coat the chicken in the flour, shaking off the excess. Dip on both sides in the eggs and coat evenly with the panko, patting the panko gently to adhere. Transfer to a platter. Let the chicken stand for about 10 minutes to set the coating.

4 Position a rack in the center of the oven and preheat the oven to 200°F/95°C. Line a large rimmed baking sheet with a wire rack.

5 Add ¼ in/6 mm oil to a very large skillet. Heat the oil over medium-high heat until shimmering. In batches without crowding, add the chicken to the oil and cook, adjusting the heat so the chicken bubbles steadily in the oil without browning too quickly, until the underside is golden brown, about 3 minutes. Turn the chicken over and brown the other side, about 3 minutes more. Transfer to the wire rack and keep warm in the oven while cooking the remaining chicken.

6 To serve, cut each chicken breast half crosswise into ½-in/12-mm strips. Transfer each to a plate and add a ramekin of the sauce for dipping. Serve with the lemon wedges.

MAKES 4 SERVINGS

The Islands are pleasantly overrun with "lunch plate" restaurants, modest establishments that specialize in saucy main courses spooned over a scoop (or two) of rice, with a side order of potato or macaroni salad. Without exception, every one of these establishments serves chicken teriyaki. Here is our recipe, which adds grilled mushrooms.

CHICKEN TERIYAKI WITH GRILLED SHIITAKE MUSHROOMS

MARINADE

⅔ cup/165 ml soy sauce

½ cup/100 g sugar

¼ cup/60 ml Chinese rice wine or dry sherry

3 green onions, white and green parts, finely chopped

1 Tbsp peeled and minced fresh ginger

3 garlic cloves, minced

4 skinless, boneless chicken breast halves, about 6 oz/170 g each

8 oz/225 g fresh shiitake mushrooms, stemmed

Vegetable oil, for brushing

1 Tbsp cornstarch

Chopped green onions, for garnish (optional)

1 To make the marinade: Whisk the ingredients together in a medium bowl to dissolve the sugar.

2 One at a time, place a chicken breast half between two plastic bags. Using the flat side of a meat pounder or a rolling pin, pound the chicken until about ½ in/12 mm thick. Pour the marinade into a 1-gl/3.8 L self-sealing plastic bag and add the chicken. Close the bag and refrigerate, turning the bag occasionally, for at least 2 or up to 8 hours.

3 Prepare an outdoor grill for direct cooking over medium heat (see page 19).

4 Remove the chicken from the marinade, reserving the marinade. Toss the shiitakes with about 2 Tbsp of the marinade in a large bowl. Arrange the chicken and mushrooms on a large rimmed baking sheet and lightly brush on both sides with the oil.

5 Brush the grill grate clean. Grill the chicken, with the lid closed as much as possible, until the undersides are seared with grill marks, about 4 minutes. Flip the chicken and add the shiitakes to the grill. Continue cooking, turning the shiitakes every few minutes, until the chicken feels firm when pressed and shows no sign of pink when pierced in the thickest part with the tip of a small, sharp knife, about 4 minutes more. Transfer the chicken and mushrooms to a platter and tent with aluminum foil to keep warm.

6 Meanwhile, sprinkle the cornstarch over ¼ cup/60 ml water in a small bowl and stir to dissolve. Strain the reserved marinade into a medium saucepan and stir in the cornstarch mixture. Bring to a boil over high heat. Reduce the heat to very low and simmer for 3 to 5 minutes. Serve the chicken and mushrooms with the sauce, sprinkled with the green onions, if you wish.

MAKES 4 SERVINGS

Here are some tips for Japanese-style grilled chicken (*yaki* means "grill," and *tori* means "chicken"). First, do not try to cook the skewers over high heat, as the deliciously sweet marinade will burn, and so will the wooden sticks holding the chicken meat. Chicken thighs will cook up juicier than breasts, and for even cooking, don't crowd the pieces of meat together. Yakitori are less substantial than kebabs, so plan on serving several per person.

CHICKEN YAKITORI

GLAZE

½ cup/120 ml soy sauce

½ cup/120 ml mirin

½ cup/120 ml sake or dry sherry

2 Tbsp sugar

4 thin slices fresh ginger

3 garlic cloves, sliced

½ tsp red pepper flakes

1 Tbsp cornstarch

1½ lb/680 g skinless, boneless chicken thighs, cut into ¾-in/2-cm pieces

Twelve 6-in/15-cm bamboo skewers, soaked in cold water for 30 minutes and drained

Vegetable oil, for brushing

1 To make the glaze: Bring the soy sauce, mirin, sake, sugar, ginger, garlic, and red pepper flakes to a boil in a medium nonreactive saucepan over high heat. Cook until the liquid is reduced to about ¾ cup/180 ml, 15 to 20 minutes. Reduce the heat to medium-low. Dissolve the cornstarch in 2 Tbsp water in a small bowl; stir into the simmering soy sauce mixture and cook until thickened, about 30 seconds. Transfer to a small bowl and let cool completely.

2 Prepare an outdoor grill for two-zone cooking over medium heat (see page 19).

3 Thread the chicken onto the skewers. Brush the chicken all over with some of the glaze. Brush with the oil. Scrub the grill grate clean. Place the skewers with the chicken directly over the heat source and the handles over the cooler area. To protect the skewers from burning (even though they have been soaked), slip a long strip of aluminum foil underneath the handles and another strip underneath the exposed pointed tips. Grill, with the lid closed as much as possible, turning the skewers occasionally and brushing with the glaze, until the chicken is opaque throughout, 15 to 20 minutes. Transfer the skewers to a platter or plates and serve.

MAKES 4 SERVINGS

Chinese roast duck sports rich meat under a crisp, glazed skin . . . is your mouth watering yet? But the trick is to render the fat that's under the skin. This recipe shares some centuries-old tricks, and while they aren't difficult, they do require several steps before roasting. Serve the duck with fried rice to get your starch and vegetables in a single side dish.

CHINESE ROAST DUCK WITH ORANGE-HONEY GLAZE

1 duck, about 4½ lb/2 kg, wing tips trimmed and giblets discarded

Finely grated zest of 1 orange

2 Tbsp fresh orange juice

2 Tbsp soy sauce

2 Tbsp honey

½ tsp Chinese five-spice powder

¼ tsp red pepper flakes

One 1-in/2.5-cm piece fresh ginger, thinly sliced

1 green onion, white and pale green parts, coarsely chopped

Orange slices, for garnish

SPECIAL EQUIPMENT: A desk fan

1 The day before roasting, bring a large pot of water to a boil over high heat. Put the duck in the sink on a wire rack. Slowly pour the boiling water all over the duck, including the back. This tightens the skin and helps the pores to release fat during roasting. Rinse the duck under cold running water and pat dry with paper towels.

2 Using the tines of a meat fork, pierce the duck all over, making sure not to reach into the flesh. Whisk the orange zest and juice, soy sauce, honey, five-spice powder, and red pepper flakes together in a small bowl. Pour into a 1-gl/3.8-L self-sealing plastic bag and add the duck. Close the bag and refrigerate, occasionally turning the bag, for at least 12 or up to 24 hours.

3 Remove the duck from the marinade and pat off the excess marinade with a paper towel. Place the duck on a roasting rack in a roasting pan. Place a desk fan near the pan and train the air flow onto the duck. Let the duck skin dry for at least 1 or up to 2 hours. (This simulates the air-drying at a Chinese market and is another trick to get crispy skin.)

4 Position a rack in the center of the oven and preheat the oven to 450°F/230°C.

5 Rinse out the roasting pan and line it with aluminum foil. Stuff the ginger and green onion into the duck's body cavity. Replace the duck on the roasting rack, breast side up. Roast for 15 minutes. Remove the duck from the oven and pierce the duck skin with the meat fork. Turn the duck over, back side up. Reduce the oven temperature to 400°F/200°C. Return the duck to the oven and roast for 15 minutes more. Turn the duck breast side up and continue roasting, occasionally piercing the duck skin and basting with the fat in the pan, until the duck is deeply browned and an instant-read thermometer inserted in the thickest part of the breast and not touching bone reads 170°F/77°C. Transfer the duck to a cutting board and let stand for 10 minutes.

6 Using a cleaver or large, heavy knife, cut the duck in half lengthwise. Cut off the drumsticks and wings. Chop each half crosswise into 4 or 5 pieces. Arrange the duck on a platter, garnish with the oranges, and serve.

MAKES 4 SERVINGS

HAWAII
6
HAWAII

With four kinds of rum, this infamous drink can easily put you into a glassy-eyed state, so approach it with caution. It is one of the faux-Polynesian drinks that put Donn Beach (of Don the Beachcomber fame) on the cocktail map and started the tiki craze in the late 1930s. The original recipe is a deeply guarded secret that Beach took to his grave, but this version is authentic enough to scare a teetotaler.

ZOMBIE

COCKTAIL

1 fl oz/30 ml gold or amber rum, such as Mount Gay Eclipse

¾ fl oz/22.5 ml white or silver rum, such as Brugal Blanco

¾ fl oz/22.5 ml triple sec or Cointreau

½ fl oz/15 ml dark rum, such as Myers's

1 fl oz/30 ml pineapple juice

1 fl oz/30 ml fresh lime juice

1 fl oz/30 ml Spiced Grapefruit Syrup (recipe follows)

Dash of Angostura bitters

¼ fl oz/7.5 ml overproof rum

SPICED GRAPEFRUIT SYRUP

½ cup/120 ml fresh grapefruit juice

½ cup/100 g superfine sugar

¼ tsp vanilla extract

Pinch of ground cinnamon

Small pinch of freshly grated nutmeg

GARNISH: **Pineapple wedge, fresh mint sprig**

1 **To make the grapefruit syrup:** Shake all of the ingredients together in a jar to dissolve the sugar. (The syrup can be refrigerated for up to 1 week.)

2 Add the cocktail ingredients to an ice-filled cocktail shaker. Shake well.

3 Fill a Belgian beer or large cognac glass with ice. Strain the cocktail into the glass. Garnish with the pineapple and mint and serve.

MAKES 1 DRINK

Why bother with Novocain when you can have a Painkiller? Even though this attitude-changing cocktail was invented in the Virgin Islands, pineapple and coconut give it a Hawaiian groove, so we have ignored geography to include it here. The number in the title refers to the ounces of rum: a No. 3 would have 3 oz/90 ml.

PAINKILLER NO. 2

2 fl oz/60 ml dark rum, preferably Pusser's British Navy Rum (see Note)

2 fl oz/60 ml pineapple juice

1 fl oz/30 ml cream of coconut

½ fl oz/15 ml fresh orange juice

GARNISH: **Freshly grated nutmeg**

1 Add the ingredients to an ice-filled cocktail shaker. Shake until well mixed.

2 Fill a large old-fashioned glass with ice. Strain the cocktail into the glass. Top with the nutmeg and serve.

MAKES 1 DRINK

NOTE: Pusser's Rum is a brand of dark, full-bodied rum, similar to the type doled out by the pusser (purser) to British sailors as part of their daily ration. The practice was abandoned in 1970.

Caramelization, a major cooking technique, works its magic in both sweet and savory dishes. Here, almost-burned sugar adds depth of flavor to a sweet and salty sauce that is a staple in Vietnamese restaurants on the Islands. Be sure to serve this with jasmine rice to soak up the sauce.

VIETNAMESE CHICKEN BREASTS WITH SAVORY CARAMEL SAUCE

CARAMEL SAUCE

¾ cup/150 g sugar

1 cup/240 ml canned reduced-sodium chicken broth

3 Tbsp Thai or Vietnamese fish sauce

3 Tbsp vegetable oil

6 skinless, boneless chicken thighs, about 1½ lb/680 g total

½ cup/70 g coarsely chopped shallots

2 Tbsp finely chopped peeled lemongrass (tender bulb only)

1 Tbsp peeled and minced fresh ginger

3 garlic cloves, minced

1 small fresh hot red chile, such as Thai, thinly sliced with seeds

Chopped fresh cilantro, for garnish

Jasmine rice, for serving

1 To make the sauce: Bring the sugar and 3 Tbsp water to a boil in a small, heavy saucepan over high heat, stirring to help dissolve the sugar. When the sugar boils, stop stirring and cook, occasionally swirling the pan by the handle, until the caramel is amber in color and very lightly smoking, about 5 minutes. (The caramel will reach about 350°F/165°C on a candy or instant-read thermometer.) Add the broth and fish sauce (take care; it will splatter) and stir until the caramel is dissolved. Remove from the heat.

2 Heat a large skillet over medium-high heat. Add 2 Tbsp of the oil and heat until the oil is very hot and shimmering. Add the chicken and cook, turning once, until browned, about 6 minutes. Transfer to a plate.

3 Add the remaining 1 Tbsp oil to the skillet. Add the shallots, lemongrass, ginger, garlic, and chile and cook, stirring often, until the shallots soften, about 1 minute. Add the sauce and bring to a boil, stirring to scrape up any browned bits in the skillet. Return the chicken to the skillet and reduce the heat to medium-low. Cover tightly and simmer until the chicken is tender and shows no sign of pink when pierced in the thickest part with the tip of a small, sharp knife, about 35 minutes. Sprinkle with the cilantro. Serve hot, with the rice.

MAKES 4 TO 6 SERVINGS

MARLIN BAR
Manhattan Island
THE FISHERMAN'S HUT

Puerto Ricans emigrated from the Caribbean in the late nineteenth century to work in the Hawaiian sugar industry. Their cuisine's empanadas can be filled with any number of sweet or savory fillings, and this chicken and bacon version is one of the best. Serve the flaky turnovers for lunch, brunch, or even a light supper with a salad. The amazingly simple pastry dough has a secret ingredient: cream cheese.

CHICKEN AND BACON EMPANADAS

DOUGH

2 cups/280 g unbleached all-purpose flour, plus more for rolling dough

1 tsp fine salt

1 cup/225 g cold unsalted butter, cut into ½-in/12-mm cubes

8 oz/225 g cream cheese, at room temperature, cut into 1-in/2.5-cm chunks

FILLING

2 slices bacon

10 oz/280 g boneless, skinless chicken thighs, cut into ⅓-in/8-mm dice

½ cup (90 g) finely chopped yellow onion

½ cup (90 g) finely chopped green bell pepper

2 garlic cloves, minced

1 Tbsp tomato paste

2 Tbsp finely chopped fresh cilantro

2 Tbsp finely chopped pimiento-stuffed green olives

2 Tbsp coarsely chopped seedless raisins

2 Tbsp rinsed and drained nonpareil capers

Kosher salt and finely ground black pepper

1 large egg, beaten until foamy

1 To make the dough: Pulse the 2 cups/280 g flour and the salt in a food processor to combine them. Add the butter and pulse a few times until the mixture looks like coarse meal with some pea-sized pieces. Add the cream cheese and pulse just until the mixture clumps together. Gather the dough into a ball. Divide in half and shape each portion into a thick disk. Wrap in plastic and refrigerate until chilled, at least 2 hours or up to 1 day.

2 To make the filling: Cook the bacon in a large skillet over medium heat, turning occasionally, until crisp and browned, about 8 minutes. Using tongs, transfer to paper towels, leaving the fat in the pan. Let cool, then coarsely crumble the bacon.

3 Return the skillet with the fat to medium heat. Add the chicken and cook, stirring occasionally, until lightly browned, about 5 minutes. Move the chicken to one side of the skillet and add the onion, bell pepper, and garlic. Cook, stirring the vegetables occasionally, until they are softened, about 3 minutes. Stir in the tomato paste and ½ cup/120 ml water. Bring to a simmer and reduce the heat to low. Cover and simmer until the chicken is tender and opaque throughout, about 25 minutes. Uncover and cook over high heat until the liquid is evaporated, about 3 minutes more. Transfer the mixture to a bowl and stir in the crumbled bacon with the cilantro, olives, raisins, and capers. Season to taste with salt and pepper. Let cool completely. (The filling can be refrigerated for up to 1 day.)

4 Divide the dough into 12 equal pieces and roll them into balls. One at a time, keeping the remaining dough refrigerated, roll the dough into a round about ⅛ in/3 mm thick. Using a saucer as a template, cut a 6-in/15-cm round from the dough, discarding the trimmings. Transfer to a plate, separating the rounds with waxed or parchment paper. Cover loosely with plastic wrap and refrigerate until ready to use, for at least 15 minutes or up to 1 day.

5 Position racks in the center and top third of the oven and preheat the oven to 350°F/180°C.

6 For each empanada, place a chilled round on a work surface. Brush the edges with beaten egg. Place 1 heaping Tbsp of the cooled filling on the bottom half of the round about ½ in/12 mm from the edge. Fold in half and seal the open edges with the tines of a fork. Pierce the top of the empanada with the fork. Place the assembled empanadas on two large rimmed baking sheets. Refrigerate until the dough is chilled, at least 10 minutes or up to 30 minutes.

7 Lightly brush the tops of the empanadas with beaten egg. Bake, switching the positions of the racks halfway through baking from top to bottom and front to back, until the empanadas are golden brown, 20 to 25 minutes. Let cool on the baking sheets until warm or at room temperature, then serve.

MAKES 12 EMPANADAS; SERVES 4 TO 6

Firewood was scarce on many Pacific Islands, so stir-frying and frying, which use small amounts of fuel, were the most common ways to cook and remain popular to this day. This sweet-and-sour dish has roots in Chinese-American cooking, though with a much lighter sauce. Of course, it is meant to be spooned over rice.

SWEET AND SOUR CHICKEN WITH MANGO AND ASPARAGUS

CHICKEN

1½ lb/680 g skinless, boneless chicken breast halves, cut into 1-in/2.5-cm pieces

1 Tbsp soy sauce

1 Tbsp Chinese rice wine or dry sherry

1 tsp sugar

1 tsp cornstarch

SAUCE

½ cup/120 ml canned reduced-sodium chicken broth

2 Tbsp soy sauce

2 Tbsp unseasoned rice vinegar

2 Tbsp Chinese rice wine or dry sherry

1 tsp sugar

1 tsp cornstarch

½ tsp red pepper flakes

3 Tbsp vegetable oil

1 lb/455 g asparagus, trimmed and cut on the diagonal into 1-in/2.5-cm pieces

4 green onions, white and green parts, cut into 1-in/2.5-cm lengths

1 Tbsp peeled and minced fresh ginger

2 garlic cloves, minced

2 mangos, pitted, peeled, and cut into 1-in/2.5-cm pieces

1 To marinate the chicken: Mix the ingredients together in a medium bowl. Let stand at room temperature for 15 to 20 minutes.

2 To prepare the sauce: Whisk the ingredients together in a small bowl to dissolve the cornstarch.

3 Heat a wok or large skillet over high heat. Add 1 Tbsp of the oil and heat until the oil is hot and shimmering. Add the asparagus and cook, stirring often, until crisp-tender, about 3 minutes. Transfer the asparagus to a platter.

4 Add 1 Tbsp of the remaining oil to the wok and heat. Add the chicken and cook, stirring often, until firm and opaque, 3 to 4 minutes. Add the chicken to the platter.

5 Add the remaining 1 Tbsp oil to the wok and heat. Add the green onions, ginger, and garlic and stir until the garlic is fragrant, about 15 seconds. Return the chicken and asparagus to the wok and add the mangos. Stir the sauce mixture to blend and stir into the wok. Bring to a boil, stirring carefully to avoid mashing the mangos. Return to the platter and serve hot.

MAKES 4 SERVINGS

A favorite on Hawaiian Chinese restaurant menus, this dish, like General Tso's chicken, seems to have been named for a historical figure (*kung pao* means "palace guardian"). Making it at home will remind you of how good freshly prepared Chinese food can be, and could discourage you from ordering takeout. Two keys to success: Use chicken thighs (which do not dry out like chicken breasts), and taste the sauce for a sharp undercurrent of vinegar.

KUNG PAO CHICKEN

CHICKEN

1 lb/455 g skinless, boneless chicken thighs, cut into 1-in/2.5-cm pieces

1 Tbsp soy sauce

1 Tbsp Chinese rice wine or dry sherry

1 Tbsp cornstarch

SAUCE

¼ cup/60 ml canned reduced-sodium chicken broth

2 Tbsp Chinese black vinegar or balsamic vinegar

1 Tbsp soy sauce

2 tsp sugar

½ tsp ground Sichuan peppercorns

1 tsp cornstarch

2 Tbsp vegetable oil

6 to 8 Chinese dried red chiles

2 green onions, white and pale green parts minced, dark green tops sliced

4 garlic cloves, minced

2 tsp peeled and minced fresh ginger

½ cup/75 g unsalted dry-roasted peanuts

1 To marinate the chicken: Toss the ingredients together in a medium bowl. Let stand at room temperature for 15 to 30 minutes.

2 To make the sauce: Mix the broth, vinegar, soy sauce, sugar, and Sichuan peppercorns together in a small bowl. Sprinkle in the cornstarch and stir to dissolve.

3 Heat a wok or large, heavy skillet over medium-high heat. Add the oil and heat until hot and shimmering. Add the chiles and stir until they turn a darker shade of red, about 15 seconds; do not burn the chiles. Add the minced green onion, the garlic, and ginger and stir until fragrant, about 15 seconds more. Add the marinated chicken and cook, stirring often, until firm and opaque throughout, 4 to 5 minutes.

4 Stir the sauce mixture to blend, stir into the skillet, and cook until boiling and thickened, about 30 seconds. Stir in the peanuts. Transfer to a serving bowl. Sprinkle with the green onion tops and serve.

MAKES 4 SERVINGS

Move over, southern-fried chicken, because you have some serious competition from this Hawaiian favorite with a teriyaki-flavored batter. The secret ingredients are sweet rice flour (mochiko) and cornstarch, neither of which absorbs oil as readily as wheat flour, resulting in an especially light crust. Allow a few hours (some cooks recommend overnight) for the marinating. This is nice with a squeeze of lemon or lime, but you won't need a sauce.

FRIED CHICKEN MOCHIKO

CHICKEN

⅓ cup/55 g sweet rice flour (mochiko)

⅓ cup/40 g cornstarch

¼ cup/50 g sugar

1 tsp kosher salt

2 large eggs, beaten

¼ cup/60 ml soy sauce

2 green onions, white and green parts, minced

1 Tbsp peeled and minced fresh ginger

2 garlic cloves, minced

2 lb/910 g boneless, skinless chicken thighs, cut into 1-in/2.5-cm pieces

Vegetable oil, for frying

1 To marinate the chicken: Whisk the rice flour, cornstarch, sugar, and salt together in a medium bowl. Make a well in the center and add the eggs, soy sauce, green onions, ginger, and garlic. Whisk to make a batter. Add the chicken and mix well. Cover and refrigerate for at least 4 or up to 24 hours.

2 Position a rack in the center of the oven and preheat the oven to 200°F/95°C. Line a large rimmed baking sheet with a wire rack. Add 2 in/5 cm oil to a large, deep saucepan and heat over high heat to 350°F/180°C on a deep-frying thermometer.

3 Working in batches and using a slotted spoon, lift the chicken from the batter, letting the excess batter drip back into the bowl, and add the chicken to the oil. Fry the chicken, turning once, until it is golden brown and cooked through, about 3 minutes. Using a wire spider or a slotted spoon, transfer the chicken to the wire rack and keep warm in the oven while frying the rest. Serve hot.

MAKES 4 SERVINGS

Vietnam's contender for the world's greatest sandwich is the bánh mì, a snack often sold at the Vietnamese restaurants scattered through the Islands. Like any sandwich, the bánh mì has many variations, but the constants are a crusty roll layered with pâté (liverwurst is just fine), meat, pickled vegetables, and cilantro. Here's a version with marinated and grilled chicken breast.

GRILLED CHICKEN BÁNH MÌ

MARINATED CHICKEN

4 boneless, skinless chicken breast halves, about 6 oz/170 g each

¼ cup/60 ml Thai or Vietnamese fish sauce

¼ cup/60 ml fresh lime juice

2 Tbsp vegetable oil

1 small fresh red chile, such as Thai, minced with seeds

2 garlic cloves, minced

PICKLED VEGETABLES

⅓ cup/75 ml rice vinegar

1 Tbsp sugar

2 tsp kosher salt

1 large carrot, peeled and cut into thin strips on a V-slicer or mandoline

½ small daikon (white radish), peeled and cut into thin strips on a V-slicer or mandoline (2 cups/250 g)

4 crusty oblong sandwich rolls, split (but not halved) lengthwise

4 Tbsp/60 ml mayonnaise

6 oz/170 g smooth liver pâté or liverwurst

¼ English (seedless) cucumber, thinly sliced

Fresh cilantro leaves, for serving

Sriracha sauce, for serving

1 **To marinate the chicken:** One at a time, place a chicken breast half between two sheets of plastic wrap. Lightly pound the chicken with the flat side of a meat pounder or a rolling pin until the chicken is about ½ in/12 mm thick. Whisk the fish sauce, lime juice, oil, chile, and garlic together in a shallow baking dish. Add the chicken, turn to coat, cover, and refrigerate for at least 1 or up to 4 hours.

2 **To pickle the vegetables:** Whisk the rice vinegar, sugar, and salt together in a medium bowl to dissolve the sugar. Add the carrot and daikon and mix well. Refrigerate for at least 1 or up to 2 hours. Drain and refrigerate until ready to serve.

3 Prepare an outdoor grill for direct cooking over medium heat (see page 19).

4 Remove the chicken from the marinade. Brush the grill grate clean. Put the chicken on the grate. Grill, with the lid closed as much as possible, turning occasionally, until the chicken feels firm when pressed, about 8 minutes. Transfer to a plate.

5 Remove some of the crumb to make a trough in each roll. Place the rolls on the grill to toast and warm, about 1 minute. Remove from the grill.

6 For each sandwich, spread the inside of the top half of a roll with 1 Tbsp of the mayonnaise. Spread about one-quarter of the pâté on the bottom half of the roll. Top with a chicken breast and as much of the pickled vegetables, cucumber slices, and cilantro as you like. Cut in half and serve with the Sriracha.

MAKES 4 SANDWICHES

Like clockwork, Hawaiian winds blow in from the sea each afternoon. They bring a breath of fresh air to each island and carry the seeds of native plants in an age-old pattern of propagation that has left a legacy of green.

Of course the wind carries the air, so essential for life as we know it. And on the wind also ride the seabirds gliding far above the coast in search of a meal. Palm trees sway in syncopation with the hula dancers, whose movements mimic those of the windblown trees. Nature inspires the art that depicts lithe dancing bodies and pays homage to the graceful swaying of indigenous plant life.

Hawaiian legend has it that Paka'a, the wind god, invented the sail. And while wind- and kite surfing did not originate on Hawaii, these two wind-driven activities have flourished here more than anywhere else. It's no wonder that the world's most renowned windsurfers call Hawaii their home.

Without the wind, the Islands' temperate climate would become oppressively hot, and the sense of freshness that pervades the atmosphere would be gone. But it would appear that Paka'a has no thoughts of abandoning his domain. Hawaii is kissed by trade winds that traverse the Pacific with great regularity. They carried the early European explorers, just as they now propel the colorful sails that lift kite surfers across the waves.

The same wind feeds the fires burning beneath Island grills. With the wind at their backs, local chefs prepare grilled dishes such as Guava-Glazed Baby Back Ribs (page 94), Grilled Tamarind Short Ribs (page 89), and Grilled Skirt Steaks with Kona Coffee Rub (page 102). But before you eat, sit back and sip a classic Mai Tai (page 167) or Singapore Sling (page 167). Watch the wind caress the trees and smell the aromas of fresh flowers riding on the breeze. This is the Hawaiian way—an easy, laid-back tradition that connects us with the elements that make life rich.

WIND

RED MEAT

Surprisingly, the Hawaiian cattle industry started in the early 1800s, and for decades, supplied the West Coast of the mainland with beef. And nothing says "Island cuisine" more than a roasted *kalua* pig, for which we give a modified version that you can easily make in your backyard.

89
GRILLED TAMARIND SHORT RIBS

90
KOREAN STEAK WITH SSAMJANG DIP

92
BRAISED PORK BELLY IN STEAMED BUNS

94
GUAVA-GLAZED BABY BACK RIBS

96
PORK ADOBO

97
ROAST PORK AND POTATOES WITH WINE AND GARLIC MARINADE

99
KALUA PULLED PORK SANDWICHES

100
LAMB SHANKS AND SNAP PEAS WITH RED CURRY SAUCE

101
HULI HULI PORK TENDERLOIN AND PINEAPPLE WITH OLD-SCHOOL TERIYAKI MARINADE

102
GRILLED SKIRT STEAKS WITH KONA COFFEE RUB

105
PANIOLO BEEF AND VEGETABLE STEW

107
PANKO-CRUSTED RACK OF LAMB WITH GREEN ONION HOISIN

108
PORK BURGERS WITH PINEAPPLE CHUTNEY AND BACON

This mouthwatering recipe guarantees succulent short ribs. First, they are leisurely braised in a tamarind-flavored broth to tenderize and infuse them with flavor. Just before serving, they are grilled to crisp them up. It is an almost primal pleasure to tear into one of these meaty ribs. Serve them with a cold, crisp salad and a sturdy red wine.

GRILLED TAMARIND SHORT RIBS

SHORT RIBS

3 Tbsp vegetable oil, plus more as needed

5 lb/2.3 kg beef short ribs on the bone (also called English cut; see Note)

1 yellow onion, coarsely chopped

1 Tbsp peeled and minced fresh ginger

4 garlic cloves, coarsely chopped

½ cup/120 ml tamarind concentrate

½ cup/120 ml Chinese rice wine or dry sherry

¼ cup/60 ml soy sauce

One 3-in/7.5-cm cinnamon stick

1 star anise pod

½ tsp red pepper flakes

GLAZE

¼ cup/60 ml hoisin sauce

2 Tbsp soy sauce

1 Tbsp Chinese rice wine or sherry

1 green onion, white and green parts, minced

1 garlic clove, crushed through a press

Vegetable oil, for brushing

1 To prepare the short ribs: Heat 2 Tbsp of the oil in a Dutch oven or flameproof casserole over medium-high heat. In batches without crowding, add the short ribs and cook, turning occasionally, and adding more oil as needed, until browned on all sides, about 6 minutes. Transfer the ribs to a platter.

2 Heat the remaining 1 Tbsp oil in the pot. Add the onion, ginger, and garlic and cook, stirring occasionally, until the onion is tender, about 3 minutes. Add the tamarind concentrate, rice wine, soy sauce, cinnamon stick, star anise, and pepper flakes and bring to a simmer, scraping up any browned bits in the bottom of the pot with a wooden spoon.

3 Return the ribs to the pot and pour in enough cold water (about 4 cups/960 ml) to barely cover the ribs. Bring to a boil and reduce the heat to medium-low. Simmer until the meat is fork-tender, about 2 hours. Remove from the heat and let the ribs stand in the liquid to cool for at least 1 or up to 2 hours. Drain the ribs, discarding the cooking liquid. (The ribs can be cooled completely, covered, and refrigerated for up to 1 day.)

4 Prepare an outdoor grill for direct cooking over medium heat (see page 19).

5 To make the glaze: Whisk the ingredients together in a small bowl.

6 Brush the grill grate clean. Lightly brush the ribs all over with oil. Grill, with the lid closed as much as possible, turning occasionally, until crisp and browned, about 10 minutes. Continue grilling and turning, brushing with the glaze, until the ribs are glazed, about 5 minutes more. Transfer to a platter. Let stand for 5 minutes and serve hot.

MAKES 6 SERVINGS

NOTE: During cooking, the bones will probably separate from the meat. If you want the "on the bone" look, the only way to keep it intact is to tie up each rib with kitchen twine before braising. Remove the twine before grilling.

The classic Korean dish bulgogi is marinated and sliced meat cooked on an indoor brazier. Here, grilled steaks are sliced and tucked into lettuce leaves with rice, kimchi, and a flavor bomb of a condiment called ssamjang. Any steak will do, but Koreans love the fatty juices of rib-eye. The pear is both a flavoring and a tenderizer for the meat.

KOREAN STEAK WITH SSAMJANG DIP

MARINADE

1 unpeeled Asian or Bosc pear, cored and coarsely chopped

½ cup/120 ml soy sauce

½ cup/120 ml Chinese rice wine or dry sherry

⅓ cup/75 ml honey

10 garlic cloves, crushed with the flat side of a knife and peeled

3 Tbsp Asian sesame oil

One 2-in/5-cm piece fresh ginger, peeled and coarsely chopped

4 green onions, white and green parts, coarsely chopped

2 Tbsp sesame seeds

3 top loin (also called strip or shell) or rib-eye steaks, about 1 lb/455 g each, cut about 1 in/2.5 cm thick

SSAMJANG

¼ cup/80 g Korean soy paste (*doenjang*) or aka miso

⅓ cup/100 g Korean chili paste (*gochujang*)

2 green onions, white and green parts, finely chopped

3 garlic cloves, minced

2 Tbsp Chinese rice wine or dry sherry

2 Tbsp soy sauce

1 Tbsp sesame seeds

18 romaine lettuce leaves

3 green onions, white and green parts, cut into 1-in/2.5-cm lengths

Cooked white rice, for serving

Homemade Kimchi (page 158) or purchased kimchi, for serving

1 To make the marinade: Process the pear, soy sauce, rice wine, honey, garlic, sesame oil, and ginger in a blender until puréed. Add the green onions and sesame seeds and pulse until the green onions are finely chopped.

2 Arrange the steaks in a large nonreactive baking dish. Pour in the marinade and cover with plastic wrap. Refrigerate, turning occasionally, for at least 3 hours or up to 12 hours. Let stand at room temperature for 1 hour before grilling.

3 To make the ssamjang: Stir the ingredients together in a medium bowl to combine. Cover and refrigerate for at least 1 hour to combine the flavors. (The ssamjang can be refrigerated for up to 1 week.)

4 Prepare an outdoor grill for direct cooking over high heat (see page 19).

5 Remove the steaks from the marinade and shake off the excess marinade. Brush the grill grate clean. Place the steaks on the grill and cook, with the lid closed as much as possible, turning once, until well browned, about 6 minutes for medium-rare. Transfer to a carving board and let stand for 3 minutes.

6 Arrange the lettuce leaves and green onions on a platter. With the knife held on a slight diagonal, slice the steaks thinly across the grain. Transfer the slices and juices to another platter. Serve with the ssamjang and bowls of the rice and kimchi. Allow each guest to make his or her own serving, with a smear of ssamjang on a lettuce leaf topped with a few slices of meat, a spoonful of rice, and kimchi and green onions, then roll the lettuce leaf up to eat.

MAKES 6 SERVINGS

Pork belly is prized by Asian cooks for its layers of meat, fat, and skin that cook slowly into a truly succulent slab of flavor. Sliced and tucked into tender buns, this is a great (if filling) way to start a party. If you don't want to steam buns at home, buy the frozen ones at an Asian market.

BRAISED PORK BELLY IN STEAMED BUNS

PORK BELLY

1 Tbsp vegetable oil

1½ lb/680 g pork belly, in one piece

1 green onion, white and green parts, coarsely chopped

1 Tbsp peeled and chopped fresh ginger

2 garlic cloves, chopped

1 Chinese dried red chile, or ½ tsp red pepper flakes

¼ cup/60 ml soy sauce

¼ cup/60 ml Chinese rice wine or dry sherry

2 Tbsp light brown sugar

One 3-in/7.5-cm cinnamon stick

1 star anise pod

1 Tbsp hoisin sauce

BUNS

1 tsp active dry yeast

1 Tbsp warm (about 110°F/43°C) water

2 cups/280 g unbleached all-purpose flour, plus more as needed

2 Tbsp granulated sugar

1 tsp baking powder

2 Tbsp whole milk

Hoisin sauce, for serving

Fresh cilantro leaves, for garnish

SPECIAL EQUIPMENT: **Triple-tiered bamboo or metal steamer**

1 **To cook the pork belly:** Heat the oil in a Dutch oven or flameproof casserole over medium-high heat. Add the pork belly and cook, turning occasionally, until browned, about 5 minutes. Transfer the pork to a plate. Add the green onion, ginger, garlic, and chile and stir until fragrant, about 15 seconds. Add the soy sauce, rice wine, brown sugar, cinnamon, and anise. Return the pork to the pot and pour in enough cold water to barely cover the pork. Bring to a boil. Reduce the heat to medium-low. Cover and simmer until the pork is fork-tender, about 2 hours. Remove from the heat and let the pork cool in the liquid.

2 Transfer the pork to a platter, cover with plastic wrap, and refrigerate until chilled, at least 2 hours or up to 2 days. Strain the braising liquid through a sieve into the pot and discard the solids in the sieve. Boil the liquid over high heat until reduced to about ⅓ cup/75 ml. Stir in the hoisin sauce. Transfer the glaze to a small bowl and let cool. (The glaze can be covered and refrigerated for up to 2 days.)

3 To make the buns: Sprinkle the yeast over the warm water in a small bowl, let stand for 5 minutes, and stir to dissolve the yeast. Mix the 2 cups/280 g flour, the sugar, and baking powder together in the bowl of a stand mixer or a large bowl. Add ½ cup/120 ml water with the yeast mixture and milk. Using the paddle attachment on low speed or a wooden spoon, mix or stir to form a soft dough. Change to the dough hook and knead on medium-low speed until the dough is smooth, adding more flour if necessary, about 6 minutes. Or, turn the dough out onto a lightly floured work surface and knead by hand until smooth, adding only enough flour to keep the dough from sticking, 6 to 8 minutes. The dough should be soft, so don't add too much flour.

4 Lightly oil a medium bowl. Shape the dough into a ball and turn the ball in the bowl to coat with oil. Cover with plastic wrap and let stand in a warm place until the dough is almost doubled in volume, about 1½ hours.

5 Divide the dough into 16 equal balls. One at a time, flatten out each ball into an oval about 4 in/6 cm long and ¼ in/6 mm thick. Fold in half crosswise, with the top half just short of meeting the bottom edge. Transfer to a baking sheet. Cover loosely with plastic wrap and let stand in a warm place while preparing the steamer.

6 Choose a large saucepan that will hold the steamer on top. Add water to a depth of 2 in/5 cm and bring to a boil over high heat. Line the bottom of each steamer tray with a round of parchment paper. Arrange the buns at least 1 in/2.5 cm apart in the trays. Place over the boiling water, cover, and steam until the buns are shiny, puffed, and cooked, about 7 minutes. Transfer the buns to a platter.

7 Position a broiler rack about 6 in/15 cm from the heat source and preheat the broiler.

8 Cut the chilled pork belly (including the skin) crosswise into ¼-in/6-mm slices, discarding any bones. Place on the broiler rack and broil, turning once, until beginning to brown, about 1 minute. Brush with some of the glaze and broil until the glaze is caramelized, about 1 minute. Turn the pork and repeat to glaze, about 2 minutes more. Transfer to a plate.

9 Serve the pork slices with the buns. Let each guest tuck pork slices into a bun and add hoisin sauce and cilantro as desired.

MAKES 4 TO 6 SERVINGS

Great ribs take time to cook to that just-right state where they are tender, juicy, and infused with smoke. This recipe delivers on that premise, with a Hawaiian-inspired guava jelly glaze enhancing the tender meat for a perfect finish. You can use guava wood, of course, but any fruitwood works well.

GUAVA-GLAZED BABY BACK RIBS

GLAZE

1 cup/335 g guava jelly or pineapple or apricot preserves

2 Tbsp soy sauce

2 Tbsp spicy brown or Dijon mustard

2 Tbsp unseasoned rice vinegar

1 Tbsp peeled and minced fresh ginger

2 garlic cloves, minced

1 tsp Sriracha sauce

RIBS

2 racks baby back ribs, about 3 lb/1.4 kg each

3 Tbsp light brown sugar

1 Tbsp kosher salt

1 tsp ground ginger

1 tsp granulated onion

1 tsp granulated garlic

1 tsp freshly ground black pepper

½ tsp cayenne pepper

2 large handfuls guava, apple, or cherry wood chips, soaked in hot water for 30 minutes and drained

1 To make the glaze: Whisk the ingredients together in a medium nonreactive saucepan. Bring to a boil over medium heat. Reduce the heat to low and simmer to reduce slightly, about 5 minutes. Transfer the glaze to a bowl and let cool completely.

2 To prepare the ribs: Slip a small, sharp knife underneath the membrane at one corner of a rack of ribs. Grab the loosened membrane with a paper towel and pull to strip it off the rack; repeat as needed until the membrane is removed. Repeat with the second rack. Cut each rack into 2 or 3 slabs.

3 Mix the brown sugar, salt, ginger, granulated onion and garlic, black pepper, and cayenne pepper together with your fingertips in a small bowl. Rub the mixture all over the ribs. Let stand at room temperature while preparing the grill.

4 Prepare an outdoor grill for indirect cooking with low heat (see page 19). For a charcoal grill, scatter half of the chips over the coals. For a gas grill, preheat the grill on high. Turn one burner off and adjust the heat on the other burner to 350°F/180°C. Place half of the chips in the grill smoker box or on a sheet of heavy-duty aluminum foil placed directly on the heat source (you may have to remove the grill grate). Let the wood burn until it smokes.

5 Brush the grill grate clean. Place the ribs on the cool side of the grill. Cook the ribs, with the lid closed, for 1 hour. Add the remaining chips to the grill. Cook, with the lid closed, until the meat has shrunk at least ¼ in/6 mm from the bone ends and the meat is so tender that it tears easily when a rack is bent in half, about 3 hours. (For a charcoal grill, add 12 briquettes to the coals about every 45 minutes to maintain the heat. You may need to leave the lid ajar for a few minutes to allow enough oxygen into the grill for the briquettes to ignite and turn gray around the edges.) Brush the tops of the ribs with some of the glaze. Cook, with the lid closed, until the glaze sets, about 5 minutes. Turn the ribs and repeat.

6 Transfer the ribs to a chopping board and let stand for 3 to 5 minutes. Cut between the bones and serve hot, with any remaining glaze.

MAKES 6 TO 8 SERVINGS

Adobo, which means "seasoning" in Spanish, could be called the national dish of the Philippines, so it gets a lot of play from Filipinos in Hawaii. With a simple ingredient list featuring pork, vinegar, and lots of garlic, it is similar to the *vinho d'alhos* on page 97, although here, the braising liquid is boiled down to make a thick sauce.

PORK ADOBO

1 Tbsp vegetable oil

2 lb/910 g skinless, boneless pork shoulder, cut into 1-in/2.5-cm cubes

¼ cup/60 ml sugarcane vinegar or unseasoned rice vinegar

¼ cup/60 ml soy sauce

6 garlic cloves, chopped

½ tsp coarsely crushed black peppercorns

3 bay leaves

Hot cooked rice, for serving

1 Heat the oil in a Dutch oven or flameproof casserole over medium-high heat. In batches without crowding, add the pork and cook, turning occasionally, until browned on all sides, about 5 minutes. Transfer to a plate. Discard the fat from the pot.

2 Return the pork to the pot and add the vinegar, soy sauce, garlic, peppercorns, and bay leaves. Bring the liquid to a boil over high heat. Reduce the heat to low and cover the pot. Simmer, stirring occasionally, until the pork is just tender, about 1¾ hours.

3 Uncover the pot and increase the heat to medium-high. Bring the cooking liquid to a boil and cook, stirring often, until reduced to a thick sauce, 5 to 10 minutes. Spoon the rice into bowls, top with the adobo, and serve.

MAKES 4 TO 6 SERVINGS

When the Portuguese came from the Azores to work in the sugar fields, they brought this recipe for *vinho d'alhos*, an assertive vinegar, wine, and garlic marinade for red meat and game. Here, pork is marinated for only a day or two, but aficionados often pickle the meat for three or even more days. The tart, spicy marinade gives the meat a pronounced, mouthwatering tang.

ROAST PORK AND POTATOES WITH WINE AND GARLIC MARINADE

MARINADE

1 cup/240 ml white wine vinegar

½ cup/120 ml dry white wine

2 Tbsp pickling spices (see Note)

4 garlic cloves, coarsely chopped

1½ tsp kosher salt

1 tsp red pepper flakes

1 bone-in pork loin roast, chine bone cracked by butcher, about 3½ lb/1.6 kg

2 lb/910 g unpeeled red potatoes, scrubbed and cut into 1½-in/4-cm chunks

1 Tbsp olive oil

Kosher salt and freshly ground black pepper

2 Tbsp chopped fresh cilantro or flat-leaf parsley, for garnish

1 At least 1 day before serving, marinate the pork: Whisk the marinade ingredients together in a large bowl. Put the pork in a 1-gl/3.8-L self-sealing plastic bag, pour in the marinade, and close the bag. Place in a baking dish and refrigerate, turning the bag occasionally, for 1 or 2 days.

2 Position a rack in the center of the oven and preheat the oven to 425°F/220°C.

3 Drain the pork and discard the marinade. Scrape off as much of the clinging spices as possible. Place the pork, bone side down, in a roasting pan. Roast for 15 minutes. Reduce the oven temperature to 350°F/180°C and continue roasting for 30 minutes more.

4 Toss the potatoes and oil together in a large bowl. Spread the potatoes around the pork and stir to coat with the pan juices. Continue roasting, occasionally stirring the potatoes, until an instant-read thermometer inserted in the center of the pork and not touching bone reads 145°F/63°C, about 1 hour. Transfer the pork to a carving board, tent with aluminum foil, and let rest for 15 to 20 minutes.

5 Return the oven temperature to 425°F/220°C. Continue roasting the potatoes, turning them occasionally with a metal spatula, until golden and tender, about 15 minutes more.

6 Carve the pork and transfer to a serving platter. Season the potatoes to taste with salt and pepper. Spread the potatoes around the pork, sprinkle with the cilantro, and serve.

MAKES 6 SERVINGS

NOTE: To substitute for the pickling spices, combine 2 tsp whole allspice, 2 tsp yellow mustard seeds, 1 tsp coriander seeds, 6 whole cloves, and 2 crumbled bay leaves.

Kalua literally means "to cook in an underground oven," but here's an above-ground way to cook the classic Island luau dish of pit-smoked pork—and serve it as an overstuffed sandwich topped with an Asian slaw. Unlike traditional barbecue with its rubs and sauces, kaula pork is relatively unseasoned, all the better to enjoy the flavor of the meat.

KALUA PULLED PORK SANDWICHES

KALUA PORK

2 boneless pork shoulder roasts, skin and butcher twine removed, about 3 lb/ 1.4 kg each (see Notes)

5 tsp kosher salt

1½ tsp freshly ground black pepper

1 thawed frozen banana leaf (see Notes), cut into 2 pieces, each about 16 in/ 40.5 cm square

12 soft sandwich rolls, split

½ recipe Guava Barbecue Glaze (page 94)

½ recipe Asian Slaw with Ginger Dressing (page 58)

2 chunks kiawe or mesquite wood or 2 large handfuls kiawe wood chips (chips only soaked in water for 30 minutes and drained; see Notes)

1 To make the pork: Season the pork all over with the salt and pepper. Wrap each roast in a banana leaf piece and overwrap with heavy-duty aluminum foil to make 2 large packets. Crimp the foil tightly at the sides so the juices won't run out of the packet during cooking. Tear open the top of the foil to expose the leaf. Let stand at room temperature while preparing the grill.

2 Prepare an outdoor grill for indirect cooking with low heat (see page 19). For a charcoal grill, let the coals burn until covered with white ash. Mound the coals on one side of the grill and let them burn until you can hold your hand about 1 in/2.5 cm above the grill grate for about 4 seconds (300°F/150°C). Place a wood chunk on the coals. For a gas grill, preheat the grill on high. Turn one burner off and adjust the heat on the other burner to 300°F/150°C. Place a wood chunk (or a handful of drained wood chips) in the grill smoker box or on a sheet of heavy-duty aluminum foil placed directly on the heat source (you may have to remove the grill grate). Let the wood burn until it smokes.

3 Place the wrapped pork on the cool side of the grill. Close the grill and cook for 45 minutes. Add another chunk of wood (or the remaining chips) to the grill (and 12 briquettes to the coals of a charcoal grill) and cook until the pork is very tender and an instant-read thermometer inserted into the center of the meat reads 190°F/88°C, about 3¼ hours more. (For a charcoal grill, add 12 briquettes to the coals about every 45 minutes to maintain the heat. You may need to leave the lid ajar for a few minutes to allow enough oxygen into the grill for the briquettes to begin to turn gray around the edges.)

4 Transfer the wrapped pork to a platter. Open the foil completely and let stand for 15 to 20 minutes. Carefully discard the foil and leaves (the juices will be hot). Transfer the pork to a carving board. Using two forks, pull the pork into shreds. Transfer the pork to a bowl and cover with foil to keep warm.

5 Divide the pork among the buns, drizzle with the glaze, and top with a spoonful of slaw. Serve immediately.

MAKES 12 SANDWICHES

NOTES: Most butchers sell boneless pork shoulder roasts. If necessary, purchase a whole pork shoulder with bones, weighing about 10 lb/4.5 kg, and ask the butcher to bone it and separate the meat into two roasts.

Kiawe (see Glossary, page 212) is plentiful on the Islands, and is the most common wood used for outdoor cooking. If you use kiawe wood chips instead of chunks, soak 2 large handfuls in hot water for 30 minutes before using. Do not soak the chunks. Not all gas grill configurations will accommodate large wood chunks, so in that case, use the easily purchased and smaller mesquite chips (every hardware store carries them).

Ti leaves are used in Hawaii to wrap the pork, but they aren't easy to find on the mainland. Banana leaves make a good substitute (see Glossary, page 211).

Hawaiian cooks know that the toughest parts of the animal are the most succulent, as seen in the wide assortment of soups and stews in the cuisine. Lamb shanks take a long, slow braise to coax to tenderness, but are well worth the wait. A creamy Thai curry sauce makes this a warming dish to spoon over rice or even mashed potatoes.

LAMB SHANKS AND SNAP PEAS WITH RED CURRY SAUCE

2 Tbsp vegetable oil

4 lamb shanks, about 1 lb/455 g each

Kosher salt and freshly ground black pepper

½ cup/75 g chopped shallots

2 Tbsp Thai red curry paste

One 14-oz/400-g can coconut milk (not cream of coconut)

1 cup/240 ml canned reduced-sodium chicken broth

2 Tbsp Thai or Vietnamese fish sauce

1 Tbsp light brown sugar

6 oz/170 g sugar snap peas

3 Tbsp finely chopped dry-roasted peanuts, for garnish

3 Tbsp finely chopped fresh Thai basil, for garnish

Lime wedges, for serving

1 Position a rack in the center of the oven and preheat the oven to 325°F/165°C.

2 Heat the oil in a Dutch oven or flameproof casserole over medium-high heat. Season the lamb with 1 tsp salt and 1 tsp black pepper. In batches, add the lamb shanks and cook, turning occasionally, until browned on all sides, about 5 minutes. Transfer the lamb to a plate.

3 Pour off all but 2 Tbsp of the fat from the pot. Add the shallots and cook, stirring often, until browned, about 1 minute. Add the curry paste and stir well. Whisk in the coconut milk, broth, fish sauce, and brown sugar. Return the lamb to the pot. Don't worry if the shanks are snug, as they will shrink during cooking. Bring the liquid to a boil.

4 Cover the pot tightly. Bake, occasionally turning the shanks, until fork-tender, about 2 hours. Remove from the oven.

5 Meanwhile, bring a medium saucepan of salted water to a boil over high heat. Add the sugar snap peas and cook until crisp-tender, about 2 minutes. Drain in a colander, rinse under cold water, and drain again. Set aside.

6 Transfer the lamb to a plate and tent with aluminum foil to keep warm. Let the cooking liquid stand for 3 minutes, then skim the fat from the surface. Bring to a boil over high heat and cook, stirring occasionally, until reduced to about 2 cups/480 ml, about 10 minutes. Season to taste with salt and pepper. Remove from the heat and stir in the sugar snap peas. Return the shanks to the pot and coat with the sauce. Divide the lamb and sauce among 4 bowls, top with a sprinkle of peanuts and basil, and serve with the lime wedges.

MAKES 4 SERVINGS

Every Hawaiian cook worth his or her pink salt has a favorite recipe for an all-purpose soy sauce marinade that they put into action for just about anything that can be grilled. It is often called huli huli ("turn, turn") sauce because the meat is flipped to keep it from burning over the coals. Before mirin and sake were readily available, many teriyaki marinades used pineapple juice as a base, and it still makes a terrific soaker.

HULI HULI PORK TENDERLOIN AND PINEAPPLE WITH OLD-SCHOOL TERIYAKI MARINADE

OLD-SCHOOL TERIYAKI MARINADE

½ cup/120 ml pineapple juice

⅓ cup/75 ml soy sauce

¼ cup/60 ml dry sherry

2 Tbsp light brown sugar

2 green onions, white and pale green parts, finely chopped

1 Tbsp peeled and minced fresh ginger

2 garlic cloves, minced

2 pork tenderloins, trimmed of excess fat and silver skin, about 1 lb/455 g each

6 fresh pineapple rings, cut about ½ in/12 mm thick

Vegetable oil, for brushing

1 To make the marinade: Whisk the ingredients together in a medium bowl to dissolve the brown sugar.

2 Place the tenderloins in a 1-gl/3.8-L self-sealing plastic bag. Pour in the marinade and close the bag. Refrigerate, turning occasionally, for at least 2 or up to 4 hours but no longer (see Note).

3 Prepare an outdoor grill for direct cooking over medium heat (see page 19).

4 Remove the pork from the marinade and wipe off the clinging solids with paper towels. Lightly brush the tenderloins and pineapple rings all over with vegetable oil. Brush the grill grate clean. Grill the pork, with the lid closed as much as possible, until it is nicely browned and an instant-read thermometer inserted in the thickest part reads 145°F/63°C, about 20 minutes. If the pork is browning too much, move it to a cooler part of the grill. Transfer the pork to a platter and tent with aluminum foil. Let stand for 5 minutes.

5 Meanwhile, add the pineapple to the grill and cook, with the lid closed as much as possible, turning once, until the pineapple is seared with grill marks and heated through, about 5 minutes. Transfer to the platter with the pork.

6 Cut the pork crosswise into slices about ½ in/12 mm thick. Cut each pineapple ring in half vertically, and serve with the pork slices.

MAKES 4 TO 6 SERVINGS

NOTE: This is a versatile marinade, but keep in mind that pineapple juice is quite acidic, and the marinade can change the food's texture if it is marinated too long. Seafood (try this marinade on swordfish or salmon) needs only 30 minutes. Boneless poultry (such as breasts) will be ready in 2 hours, and pork tenderloin and chops in no longer than 4 hours. Sturdier cuts of meat, such as steaks and spareribs, can be marinated for up to 6 hours.

Hawaii is the only U.S. state with the weather and topography suitable for growing coffee, and while Kona is the best known, every island has its own crop. You may be surprised to find that ground coffee is also the base for an interesting and very tasty steak rub. Serve this with a simple side dish, such as Asparagus with Oyster Sauce (page 168), so you can really savor the spicy flavor of the steak.

GRILLED SKIRT STEAKS WITH KONA COFFEE RUB

RUB

1½ Tbsp kosher salt

1 Tbsp finely ground Kona coffee

1 Tbsp sweet paprika, preferably Spanish or Hungarian

1 tsp freshly ground black pepper

1 tsp ground cumin

¼ tsp cayenne pepper

2½ lb/1.2 kg skirt steaks, cut into serving pieces

Extra-virgin olive oil

1 **To make the rub:** Whisk the ingredients together in a small bowl.

2 Lightly coat the steaks on both sides with the oil. Generously sprinkle the steaks all over with the rub and gently massage it in. Let the steaks stand at room temperature for 20 to 30 minutes.

3 Prepare a grill for direct cooking over high heat (see page 19).

4 Brush the grill grate clean. Cook the steaks over direct high heat, with the lid closed as much as possible, flipping the steaks halfway through cooking, until well browned, about 6 minutes for medium-rare. Transfer the steaks to a carving board and let stand for 3 to 5 minutes. With the knife held on a slight diagonal, carve the steaks across the grain. Transfer the slices and juices to a platter and serve hot.

MAKES 4 TO 6 SERVINGS

This rib-sticking stew is similar to what was served from huge cauldrons to feed hungry *paniolos* (cowboys) on the Big Island before the industry declined in the 1930s (although Parker Ranch, established in 1847, is still going strong). It's an Island version of a Western dish, with Asian touches supplied by Chinese ranch cooks.

PANIOLO BEEF AND VEGETABLE STEW

4 Tbsp/60 ml vegetable oil, plus more as needed

3-lb/1.4-kg boneless beef chuck, cut into 1½-in/4-cm chunks

Kosher salt and freshly ground black pepper

⅓ cup/45 g all-purpose flour

1 large yellow onion, chopped

2 Tbsp peeled and minced fresh ginger

4 garlic cloves, minced

2 cups/480 ml canned reduced-sodium beef broth

2 Tbsp tomato paste

2 Tbsp soy sauce

3 carrots, peeled and cut into ½-in/12-mm rounds

3 celery stalks, cut into ½-in/12-mm slices

2 baking potatoes, peeled and cut into 1-in/2.5-cm cubes

Hot cooked rice, for serving

Chopped fresh cilantro, for garnish (optional)

1 Position a rack in the center of the oven and preheat the oven to 350°F/180°C.

2 Heat 2 Tbsp of the oil in a Dutch oven or flameproof casserole over medium-high heat. Season the beef with 1½ tsp salt and 1 tsp pepper. In batches, toss the beef in the flour and shake off the excess. Add to the pot and cook, stirring occasionally, adding more oil as needed, until the beef is browned, about 5 minutes. Transfer to a plate.

3 Add the remaining 2 Tbsp oil to the pot and heat. Add the onion, ginger, and garlic and cook, stirring occasionally and scraping up the browned bits in the pot with a wooden spoon, until the onion softens, about 3 minutes. Add the broth, tomato paste, and soy sauce and mix well. Return the beef to the pot with the carrots, celery, and potatoes. Add cold water (about 4 cups/960 ml) to barely cover the ingredients. Bring to a boil.

4 Cover and bake until the meat is very tender, 1½ to 1¾ hours. Season to taste with salt and pepper. (If you would like a thicker sauce, use a slotted spoon to transfer the beef and vegetables to a serving bowl and cover with aluminum foil to keep warm. Return the pot to medium-high heat and bring to a boil. Cook, whisking often to avoid scorching, until the sauce is reduced by one-quarter, about 5 minutes. Pour over the meat and vegetables.) Serve the stew over rice, sprinkled with cilantro, if using.

MAKES 6 SERVINGS

Home on the Volcano

Hawaiian cowboys? Many people are surprised to learn about the Big Island's cattle ranches, which date back nearly two centuries ago, when King Kamehameha III brought over Mexican *vaqueros* to handle the wild herds that were out of control. (*Paniolo* derives from the word *español*, or Spanish, the *vaqueros'* language.) Cattle became an industry, with the establishment of huge ranches where the cattle fed on newly introduced grasses and the pods of the kiawe tree.

Many a restaurant has made its reputation on rack of lamb, but it is surprisingly easy to make at home. This recipe combines Asian techniques and ingredients for a dish that you will turn to again and again when planning a dinner party. Wasabi–Roasted Garlic Mashed Potatoes (page 161) and Sesame and Ginger Spinach (page 165) would be perfect side dishes.

PANKO-CRUSTED RACK OF LAMB WITH GREEN ONION HOISIN

MARINADE

¼ cup/60 ml soy sauce

¼ cup/60 ml Chinese rice wine or dry sherry

3 Tbsp hoisin sauce

1½ Tbsp honey

3 garlic cloves, coarsely chopped

¼ tsp red pepper flakes

2 racks of lamb, Frenched and trimmed, about 1¾ lb/800 g each

1 Tbsp vegetable oil

2 Tbsp hoisin sauce

1 green onion, white and green parts, minced

½ cup/45 g panko (Japanese bread crumbs)

1 To marinate the lamb: Whisk the ingredients together in a medium bowl with 3 Tbsp water. Pour into a 1-gl/3.8-L self-sealing plastic bag. Add the lamb, close the bag, and refrigerate, turning the bag occasionally, for at least 1 or up to 4 hours. Remove the lamb from the marinade, discarding the marinade, and pat dry with paper towels.

2 Position a rack in the bottom third of the oven and preheat the oven to 400°F/200°C.

3 Heat the oil in a large skillet over high heat. Using kitchen tongs, add the lamb racks and cook, turning and holding the racks in place as needed, until the meaty areas are lightly browned, about 2 minutes. Transfer the lamb to a plate. Mix the hoisin sauce and green onion together in a small bowl. Spread the hoisin mixture in a thin, even layer over the meaty top of each rack. Sprinkle and coat the hoisin coating with the panko, patting to help it adhere. Place the lamb racks, panko sides up, on a large rimmed baking sheet.

4 Roast until an instant-read thermometer inserted in the thickest part of a rack and not touching bone reads 125°F/50°C for medium-rare, about 20 minutes. Transfer to a carving board and let stand for 5 minutes.

5 Carve each lamb rack between the bones to yield 16 chops. For each serving, arrange 4 chops on a dinner plate. Serve at once.

MAKES 4 SERVINGS

Everyone loves a good beef burger, but when you want to mix things up a bit, try this pork burger with Hawaiian flavors. It has two (count 'em) "secret sauces": a sweet-and-tangy pineapple chutney and a spicy Sriracha mayonnaise. To cook the burgers all the way through without burning, be sure to use a medium fire and keep the grill lid closed.

PORK BURGERS WITH PINEAPPLE CHUTNEY AND BACON

PINEAPPLE CHUTNEY

2 cups/380 g ¼-in/6-mm-diced fresh pineapple

½ cup/65 g chopped red bell pepper

½ cup/75 g chopped yellow onion

⅓ cup/75 ml unseasoned rice vinegar

⅓ cup/65 g packed light brown sugar

1 Tbsp peeled and minced fresh ginger

1 tsp dry mustard

1 small fresh red chile, such as Thai or serrano, seeded and minced

1 star anise pod

1 garlic clove, minced

½ tsp kosher salt

SRIRACHA MAYONNAISE

½ cup/120 ml mayonnaise

2 Tbsp tomato ketchup

1 tsp Sriracha or chili garlic paste

PORK BURGERS

2 lb/910 g ground pork

2 green onions, white and green parts, minced

3 garlic cloves, crushed through a press

2 Tbsp soy sauce

1 tsp kosher salt

1 tsp freshly ground black pepper

Vegetable oil, for brushing

6 soft hamburger buns

6 slices bacon, halved crosswise and cooked until crisp

6 red lettuce leaves

1 To make the chutney: Bring the ingredients to a boil in a nonreactive saucepan over high heat, stirring to dissolve the sugar. Reduce the heat to medium-low and cook, stirring occasionally, until the juices have reduced by half, about 20 minutes. Increase the heat to high and cook, stirring often, until the juices have evaporated, about 5 minutes. Transfer the chutney to a bowl and let cool. Discard the star anise. (The chutney can be covered and refrigerated for up to 3 days. Remove from the refrigerator 1 hour before serving.)

2 To make the mayonnaise: Stir the ingredients together in a small bowl. Cover and refrigerate until ready to use.

3 To make the burgers: Mix the ingredients together in a medium bowl just until combined. Shape into 6 patties, each about 3½ in/9 cm in diameter. Make a deep, wide indentation in each burger to keep it from shrinking into a dome during cooking. Refrigerate the patties until ready to cook.

4 Prepare an outdoor grill for direct cooking over medium-high heat (see page 19).

5 Brush the grill grate clean. Lightly brush the burgers with oil on both sides. Grill the burgers, with the lid closed as much as possible, turning them once, until they feel firm when pressed, 8 to 10 minutes. Transfer to a plate and let stand for 3 minutes. Toast the buns on the grill, about 1 minute.

6 For each burger, spread the cut sides of a bun with some of the mayonnaise. Place a burger on the bottom half and top with 1 spoonful of chutney, 2 bacon halves, and a lettuce leaf. Add the bun top and serve.

MAKES 6 BURGERS

Keoki Wood grew up in Hawaii, the son of a commercial airline pilot. But even as a boy, his aspirations were more down to earth than those of his father. Keoki started raising livestock when he was in grammar school, and after high school he worked on a number of local cattle ranches. In 2002, he was hired by Parker Ranch to be a "cow boss," as he calls himself. The rancher manages a crew of 11 cowboys, who canvas 130,000 acres as they watch over 10,000 cattle. "It's a big job," Keoki says. "But I love it."

The cowboys rarely leave their saddles. They herd cattle, sort calves, and traverse the rugged terrain in a time-honored fashion stretching back two centuries. The stock at Parker Ranch grew out of a small herd—five cows—brought to Hawaii in 1788 by a British sea captain. By the mid-1800s, the ranch had been established by an enterprising young sailor from Massachusetts, John Palmer Parker, who originally jumped ship in 1809 to start a new life on the lush hillsides of his new Hawaiian home.

Keoki says, in his understated way, "We're in the grass business. We use cattle to harvest the grass, and we sell the cattle for revenue." Quite a bit is sold locally, too. If you've ever ordered a hamburger in Hawaii, there's a good chance it was made with Parker Ranch beef. The cowboys preside over a pristine mountain environment, at an altitude where steady rainfall and moderate year-round temperatures provide perfect pasture for grass-fed cattle.

Mornings on the ranch begin at 6:30. As Keoki saddles up, he can smell the moist air, the fresh grass, and the rich earth of the land. "This is a bit of paradise," says the cow boss. "I'm lucky to be here every day."

PARKER RANCH, WAIMEA

SEAFOOD

The warm Pacific waters around Hawaii teem with fish that provide good eating for the Islands; swordfish, tuna, mahi mahi, snapper, and sea bass are just a few of the beloved local species. The ocean waters are too warm here for some of the shellfish that thrive in cold temperatures, but excellent farms provide shrimp and other seafood for local chefs and cooks.

115
MAHI MAHI WITH MACADAMIA NUT CRUST AND PAPAYA SALSA

116
SHRIMP AND SCALLOPS IN THAI CURRY SAUCE

118
STEAMED SEA BASS WITH GINGER DIPPING SAUCE

121
TOGARASHI-SESAME SNAPPER WITH SAKE AND LIME SAUCE

123
SALMON FILLETS WITH GINGER GLAZE

124
GRILLED SWORDFISH WITH ORANGE-MISO MARINADE

127
AHI TUNA WITH LEMONGRASS CRUST AND SWEET CHILI–MUSTARD SAUCE

128
PORTUGUESE SEAFOOD AND SAUSAGE STEW

Until fairly recently, most of the food visitors ate in Hawaii did not begin to reflect the beautiful bounty that the Islands has to offer. That changed dramatically when classically trained chefs began to combine their knowledge with local ingredients to create New Hawaiian Cuisine. This dish has become an icon of the genre. Broccolini with Chile-Lemon Oil (page 170) would be a great accompaniment.

MAHI MAHI WITH MACADAMIA NUT CRUST AND PAPAYA SALSA

PAPAYA SALSA

2 Tbsp fresh lime juice

1 Tbsp light brown sugar

1 Tbsp minced shallot

1 Tbsp minced fresh cilantro

1 Tbsp finely chopped crystallized ginger

1 tsp Sriracha or other red pepper sauce

1 garlic clove, minced

1 cup/170 g ½-in/12-mm-diced papaya

MAHI MAHI

½ cup/55 g unsalted macadamia nuts

½ cup/45 g panko (Japanese bread crumbs)

4 mahi mahi fillets, without skin, about 6 oz/170 g each

¾ tsp kosher salt

½ tsp freshly ground black pepper

1 large egg white, beaten until foamy

1 Tbsp unsalted butter

2 Tbsp vegetable oil

1 To make the salsa: Mix the lime juice, brown sugar, shallot, cilantro, ginger, Sriracha, and garlic together in a medium bowl to dissolve the brown sugar. Mix in the papaya. Cover and refrigerate until ready to serve, up to 4 hours.

2 To prepare the mahi mahi: Pulse the macadamia nuts in a food processor until very finely chopped, taking care not to turn them into nut butter. Transfer to a shallow dish and mix with the panko.

3 Season the fish with the salt and pepper. Lightly brush the fish all over with the beaten egg white. Coat the fish with the panko mixture, patting it on to help it adhere. Transfer to a baking sheet and let stand for 10 minutes to help set the coating.

4 Melt the butter with the oil in a very large nonstick skillet over medium heat. Add the mahi mahi and cook, adjusting the heat as needed so the crust doesn't brown too quickly, until the underside is golden brown, 3 to 4 minutes. Flip the mahi mahi over and continue cooking until the other side is browned, about 3 minutes longer. Transfer each fillet to a dinner plate. Serve with the papaya salsa.

MAKES 4 SERVINGS

There are about eight different spices in traditional Indian curry powder, while Thai curry paste adds such aromatic solids as red chiles, ginger, lemongrass, and garlic. Combine the two types of curry flavoring, and you have a dish fit for the cooking gods. Be careful not to overcook the seafood in the initial browning, because it will be reheated in the sauce.

SHRIMP AND SCALLOPS IN THAI CURRY SAUCE

3 Tbsp vegetable oil

12 large sea scallops, adductor muscle removed

24 extra-large (26 to 30 count) shrimp, peeled and deveined

2 Tbsp minced peeled lemongrass (tender bulb only)

2 Tbsp peeled and minced fresh ginger

1 Tbsp Thai red curry paste

1 tsp Madras-style curry powder

1 cup/240 ml canned reduced-sodium chicken broth

1 cup/240 ml canned coconut milk (not cream of coconut)

2 tsp light brown sugar

Kosher salt

Cooked jasmine rice, for serving

1 Heat 1 Tbsp of the oil in a very large nonstick skillet over medium-high heat until the oil is very hot but not smoking. Add the scallops and cook, turning once, until browned on both sides but still translucent in the center, about 5 minutes. Transfer the scallops to a platter.

2 Heat 1 Tbsp of the remaining oil in the skillet until very hot but not smoking. Add the shrimp and cook, turning them once, just until they turn pink and are slightly undercooked, 2 to 2½ minutes. Add the shrimp to the platter.

3 Heat the remaining 1 Tbsp oil in the skillet. Add the lemongrass and ginger and stir until fragrant, about 30 seconds. Add the red curry paste and curry powder and stir well for another 30 seconds. Add the broth, coconut milk, and brown sugar and bring to a boil, scraping up the browned bits in the bottom of the skillet with a wooden spoon. Reduce the heat to medium and boil, stirring often, until the sauce is thickened and reduced by about two-thirds, 8 to 10 minutes. During the last minute or so, pour the liquid that has collected on the platter into the sauce.

4 Add the scallops and shrimp to the sauce, bring to a boil, and cook just until the seafood is cooked through, about 1 minute. Season to taste with salt. Transfer the curry to the platter and serve with jasmine rice.

MAKES 4 TO 6 SERVINGS

This Chinese recipe of steamed fish with a ginger-scented dipping sauce has a lot going for it. It is ready for serving in no time, and its low-fat profile is perfect for when you are counting calories . . . or even when you are not. But its main asset is its flavor, as steaming gently cooks the fish to retain its moisture and texture. This technique works well with other firm-fleshed varieties such as grouper.

STEAMED SEA BASS WITH GINGER DIPPING SAUCE

3 Tbsp soy sauce

1 Tbsp Chinese rice wine or dry sherry

1 Tbsp Asian sesame oil

2 green onions, white and green parts, julienned

One 2-in/5-cm piece fresh ginger, peeled and julienned

1 garlic clove, minced

4 skinless sea bass fillets, about 6 oz/170 g each

SPECIAL EQUIPMENT: **Bamboo or metal steamer**

1 Mix the soy sauce, rice wine, sesame oil, half of the green onions, half of the ginger, and the garlic with 2 Tbsp water in a small bowl. Divide the dipping sauce evenly among 4 small ramekins.

2 Choose a large saucepan that will hold a steamer on top. Add 2 in/5 cm water and bring to a boil over high heat. If using a metal steamer, lightly oil the rack.

3 Place the fillets in the steamer. If they are too large to fit easily, fold each in half from tip to tip. Top each fillet with equal amounts of the remaining green onions and ginger. Place the steamer over the saucepan and cover tightly. Steam over high heat until the fish is opaque when flaked in the thickest part with the tip of a small, sharp knife, 8 to 10 minutes.

4 Transfer each fillet to a dinner plate and serve with the dipping sauce.

MAKES 4 SERVINGS

Many Japanese diners carry a small bottle of *togarashi*, a bracingly hot and savory spice mixture, to season their food, just as some Americans might travel with their own hot pepper sauce. This blend is an excellent seasoning for snapper fillets, which are served with an elegant sake and lime butter sauce that would also be fine with a side of steamed asparagus or sugar snap peas.

TOGARASHI-SESAME SNAPPER WITH SAKE AND LIME SAUCE

SAUCE

1 lime

1 cup/240 ml good-quality sake, such as Gekkeikan Traditional

2 Tbsp chopped shallots

¾ cup/170 g cold unsalted butter, cut into ½-in/12-mm cubes

Kosher salt and freshly ground white pepper

SNAPPER

1½ tsp *togarashi* (Japanese seven-spice blend)

1 Tbsp sesame seeds, preferably half black sesame

4 snapper fillets with skin, about 6 oz/170 g each

1 Tbsp vegetable oil

1 To make the sauce: Finely grate the zest from the lime and reserve the zest. Juice the lime; you should have 3 Tbsp.

2 Bring the sake, shallots, and lime juice to a boil in a small nonreactive saucepan over high heat. Boil until the liquid has reduced to about 2 Tbsp, about 7 minutes. Reduce the heat to very low. A few cubes at a time, whisk in the butter. The butter should not actually melt, but soften into an emulsified sauce with the shallot mixture. Occasionally remove the saucepan from the heat so the butter doesn't melt. Strain the sauce into a small bowl. Stir in the zest and season to taste with salt and pepper. To keep the sauce warm, place the bowl in a small skillet of hot water over very low heat. The sauce will keep warm for about 20 minutes. Whisk well before serving.

3 To prepare the snapper: Mix the *togarashi* and sesame seeds together in a small bowl. Season the flesh side of the snapper with the sesame mixture, patting the mixture on to help it adhere.

4 Heat the oil in a very large nonstick skillet over medium heat. Add the snapper, flesh side down, and cook until the underside is lightly browned, about 3 minutes. Flip the snapper and cook until the other side is browned and the fish is just opaque when flaked in the thickest part with the tip of a small, sharp knife, about 3 minutes more.

5 Transfer each fish to a dinner plate. Spoon the sauce around the fish and serve immediately. (Leftover sauce can be cooled, covered, and refrigerated for up to 2 days. Let the sauce stand at room temperature for about 30 minutes before spooning over hot green vegetables. The heat of the vegetables will melt the sauce. It may not be smooth, but it will taste fine.)

MAKES 4 SERVINGS

There isn't a lot of salmon in Hawaii (the salted fish in lomi-lomi salmon, one of the most beloved local recipes, was originally shipped in from the Pacific Northwest), but the local wild fish is of very high quality. This recipe counterpoints the rich flesh with a ginger glaze. Smart cooks know that when you want dinner in a hurry, fish is a good solution, and this recipe is a perfect example of that axiom.

SALMON FILLETS WITH GINGER GLAZE

¼ cup/60 ml hoisin sauce

2 Tbsp Chinese rice wine or dry sherry

1 green onion, white and pale green parts minced, and dark green leaves sliced

1 small garlic clove, crushed through a press

2 Tbsp shredded unpeeled fresh ginger (use the large holes of a box grater)

4 salmon fillets, each 6 oz/170 g, skinned and pinbones removed

Toasted sesame seeds, for garnish

1 Position an oiled broiler rack 6 in/15 cm from the heat source and preheat the broiler.

2 Mix the hoisin sauce, rice wine, minced green onion, and garlic in a small bowl. Working over the bowl, squeeze the ginger hard in your hand to extract the juice, and stir the juice into the sauce. Discard the ginger.

3 Broil the fillets, skinned side up, for 3 minutes. Flip the salmon over. Slather with the glaze and continue broiling until the glaze is bubbling, 2 to 3 minutes for medium-rare salmon. Transfer each fillet to a dinner plate. Sprinkle with the sliced green onion leaves and sesame seeds and serve.

MAKES 4 SERVINGS

Swordfish teems in the water around the Islands, and the locals call it *a'uku*. This firm fish can take on bold seasonings, like this marinade of miso balanced with sweet orange juice (it is also good with salmon). As an alternative, try the Old-School Teriyaki Marinade on page 101. Serve this with a simple vegetable, such as sautéed snow peas with sesame seeds.

GRILLED SWORDFISH WITH ORANGE-MISO MARINADE

ORANGE-MISO MARINADE

¼ cup/75 g white miso

Finely grated zest of 1 orange

¼ cup/60 ml fresh orange juice

3 Tbsp sugar

3 Tbsp mirin

3 Tbsp sake, such as Gekkeikan Traditional

4 swordfish steaks, about 6 oz/170 g each and cut about 1 in/2.5 cm thick

Vegetable oil, for brushing

1 To make the marinade: Whisk the ingredients together in a medium bowl to dissolve the sugar.

2 Put the swordfish in a 1-gl/3.8 L self-sealing plastic bag. Pour in the marinade and close the bag. Refrigerate, occasionally turning the bag, for at least 1 or up to 2 hours.

3 Prepare an outdoor grill for direct cooking over medium heat (see page 19).

4 Remove the swordfish from the marinade and pat off the excess marinade with paper towels. Lightly brush the swordfish on both sides with the oil. Brush the grill grate clean. Grill the swordfish, with the lid closed as much as possible, until the underside is seared with grill marks, about 3 minutes. Flip the swordfish over and continue grilling, with the lid closed, until the fish is barely opaque when pierced in the center with the tip of a small, sharp knife, 3 to 5 minutes more. Transfer to plates and serve hot.

MAKES 4 SERVINGS

In Hawaii, *ahi* refers specifically to the yellow fin and bigeye varieties of tuna (albacore is called *ahi tombu*). World War II effectively squelched the thriving Hawaiian canned tuna industry, but fresh tuna is savored in recipes like this one, based on a Tommy Bahama favorite, which takes minutes to prepare and yields professional results.

AHI TUNA WITH LEMONGRASS CRUST AND SWEET CHILI–MUSTARD SAUCE

SAUCE

½ cup/120 ml Asian sweet chili sauce

1 Tbsp stone-ground mustard

1½ tsp unseasoned rice vinegar

1½ tsp soy sauce

CRUST

¼ cup/20 g coarsely chopped peeled lemongrass (tender bulb only)

¾ cup/60 g panko (Japanese bread crumbs)

2 Tbsp minced fresh cilantro

4 top-quality tuna steaks, 6 oz/170 g each and about 1½ in/4 cm thick

Vegetable oil for brushing, plus 2 Tbsp

1 tsp kosher salt

¼ tsp freshly ground black pepper

Sesame seeds, for garnish

1 To make the sauce: Whisk the ingredients together in a medium bowl.

2 To make the crust: Process the lemongrass in a food processor until very finely minced—the initial chopping by hand won't be fine enough. Transfer to a medium bowl and stir in the panko and cilantro.

3 Lightly brush the tuna all over with oil. Season the tuna with the salt and pepper, then coat on all sides with the crust, patting it on to help it adhere. Let stand for 5 minutes.

4 Heat the 2 Tbsp oil in a very large nonstick skillet over medium heat. Add the tuna and cook until the crust on the underside is golden brown, about 3 minutes. Flip the tuna and cook until the crust on the other side is golden brown, about 3 minutes more. Transfer each tuna steak to a dinner plate and spoon the sauce around the tuna. Sprinkle with the sesame seeds and serve.

MAKES 4 SERVINGS

A *cataplana* is both a Portuguese spherical metal cooking vessel and the seafood stew cooked in the pot. The pot lid clamps shut to contain the cooking juices, but a large Dutch oven with a tight-fitting lid works equally well. Pork and seafood are a beloved combination in Portuguese cooking. Don't forget to serve lots of crusty bread with the cataplana—you won't want to waste a drop of the sauce.

PORTUGUESE SEAFOOD AND SAUSAGE STEW

36 Manila clams or 24 littleneck clams

1 Tbsp olive oil

5 oz/140 g smoked spicy sausage, such as linguiça or chorizo, cut into ½-in/12-mm dice

1 yellow onion, finely chopped

2 garlic cloves, minced

1 bay leaf

¼ tsp red pepper flakes

¼ cup/60 ml dry white wine

½ cup/125 g crushed tomatoes

1 lb/455 g jumbo (21 to 25 count) shrimp, peeled and deveined

Kosher salt and freshly ground black pepper

2 Tbsp chopped fresh cilantro

1 Soak the clams in cold salted water for 1 hour. Drain and scrub well under cold running water.

2 Heat the oil in a large Dutch oven or flameproof casserole over medium-high heat. Add the sausage and cook, stirring occasionally, until lightly browned, about 2 minutes. Add the onion, garlic, bay leaf, and pepper flakes. Cook, stirring often, until the onion softens, about 2 minutes.

3 Stir in the wine and boil until reduced by half, about 2 minutes. Stir in the tomatoes and bring to a boil. Add the clams and cover tightly. Cook for 5 minutes. Scatter the shrimp over the clams and cover again. Cook, occasionally shaking the pot, until the clams open and the shrimp are opaque, 3 to 5 minutes more. Discard any unopened clams.

4 Season the stew to taste with salt and pepper. Divide the stew among 4 deep soup bowls, discarding the bay leaf. Sprinkle with the cilantro and serve.

MAKES 4 SERVINGS

Hawaii was created by fire: powerful volcanic eruptions that emerged from the seabed a million years ago and grew into submarine mountains. Only the peaks of the mountains emerge from the ocean. Separated by an azure sea, these mountaintops form the chain of eight islands known collectively as the state of Hawaii.

Mount Haleakala, on the island of Maui, is one of the tallest mountains on Earth, though much of it exists below water. According to local lore, the crater at the top of the volcano was home to the grandmother of the demigod Maui. Legend has it that she helped Maui capture the sun and direct its passage across the sky. It's no wonder that the word *haleakala* means "house of the sun." Although there has been no eruption on Mount Haleakala for centuries, it is still considered to be active.

Other Hawaiian volcanoes have more recently displayed their fiery personalities. On the island of Hawaii, Mauna Loa last erupted in 1984, and Kilauea has been continuously erupting since 1983. Over time, what was once hot lava cooled enough to become the basis for fertile soil, basalt basins for freshwater lagoons, and an idyllic landscape now home to those lucky enough to live here.

The numerous recipes for grilled foods in this book will provide you with many opportunities to experience the primal pleasure of cooking on an open fire. One of Hawaii's most famous culinary traditions is *kalua*, which means cooking in an underground oven called an *imu*. Classic dishes like *kalua* pig are the centerpieces of a festive Hawaiian luau, or feast. But we don't expect you to dig up your backyard for a luau at home. Instead, try our Kalua Pulled Pork Sandwiches (page 99) for a taste of *imu*-style cooking—no shovel required!

Both the sun and the earth's core produce fires that heat our planet and shape our world. The fire in your stove, grill, or hearth is added testament to this element's special nature—a centerpiece for living well.

FIRE

NOODLES AND RICE

Hawaiians love noodles so much that many people consider saimin (similar to ramen) to be the state dish. Here is a collection of Hawaiian recipes that use a variety of noodles in the Asian tradition. Most have a homemade broth base, but you can make the broth ahead and freeze it to use as needed. Also included are main-course fried rice dishes that are perfect for supper or lunch.

135
CHICKEN CHOW FUN WITH SUGAR SNAP PEAS AND SHIITAKES

136
KOREAN CELLOPHANE NOODLES WITH CHICKEN AND VEGETABLES

141
FRIED RICE WITH KIMCHI, BACON, AND PEAS

142
GARLIC FRIED RICE WITH SAUSAGE, EGGS, AND GREEN ONIONS

143
CHINATOWN CHOW MEIN WITH PORK AND MUSHROOMS

144
VIETNAMESE NOODLE SOUP WITH BEEF

147
PAN-COOKED NOODLES WITH SHRIMP AND CHORIZO (*PANCIT*)

149
SAIMIN WITH ASIAN CHICKEN BROTH

150
PORK RAMEN WITH SHOYU BROTH

Chow fun is a member of the lo mein family, although it uses rice noodles instead of the wheat variety. Because they are perishable and delicate, fresh rice noodles are not easy to find, even at Asian markets, but the dried ones work very well. The sauce uses the robust flavors of oyster sauce, black bean sauce, and rice wine to season the bland noodles.

CHICKEN CHOW FUN WITH SUGAR SNAP PEAS AND SHIITAKES

MARINATED CHICKEN

12 oz/340 g skinless, boneless chicken breast halves

1 Tbsp soy sauce

1 tsp Chinese rice wine or dry sherry

2 tsp cornstarch

1 tsp Asian sesame oil

½ tsp brown sugar

7 oz/200 g wide rice noodles

1 tsp Asian sesame oil

2 Tbsp oyster sauce

1 Tbsp black bean sauce

1 Tbsp Chinese rice wine or dry sherry

3 Tbsp vegetable oil

6 large shiitake mushrooms, stemmed and sliced

4 oz/115 g sugar snap peas

1 small yellow onion, cut into thin half-moons

3 green onions, white and green parts, chopped into 1-in/2.5-cm pieces

2 garlic cloves, minced

2 tsp peeled and minced fresh ginger

1 To marinate the chicken: Holding a large knife at a slight diagonal, cut the chicken across the grain into slices about ¼ in/6 mm thick. Cut the slices into pieces about 2 in/5 cm long. Transfer the chicken to a medium bowl. Add the soy sauce, rice wine, cornstarch, sesame oil, and brown sugar and mix well. Let stand for about 20 minutes.

2 Meanwhile, put the noodles in a large bowl and add hot water to cover. Soak the noodles, stirring occasionally, until they are softened but slightly chewy, 10 to 15 minutes. Drain well and toss with the sesame oil.

3 Whisk the oyster sauce, black bean sauce, rice wine, and 1 Tbsp water together in a small bowl.

4 Heat a large wok or skillet over medium-high heat. Add 1 Tbsp of the oil and heat until hot but not smoking. Add the chicken and its marinade and cook, stirring occasionally, until the chicken is opaque when pierced in the center with the tip of a sharp knife, 2 to 3 minutes. Transfer the chicken to a platter.

5 Add the remaining 2 Tbsp oil to the wok. Add the mushrooms, sugar snap peas, and yellow onion and cook, stirring often, until the vegetables soften, about 1 minute. Add the green onions, garlic, and ginger and stir until fragrant, about 15 seconds. Add the noodles. Cook, tossing the noodles often, until they are hot, 1 to 2 minutes. Return the chicken to the wok, add the oyster sauce mixture, and toss the noodles to coat with the sauce. Transfer the chow fun to the platter and serve.

MAKES 4 SERVINGS

The slippery transparent noodles served everywhere in Hawaii go by many names, including saifun and bean threads. Locals usually call them long rice, even though they are made from mung beans, because they are often served, like rice, as a plain side dish. Here, the noodles are an ingredient in *chapchae*, a full-flavored Korean dish loaded with fresh vegetables and served as a main course. As with all stir-fries, prepare everything before you start, and the final cooking will be a breeze.

KOREAN CELLOPHANE NOODLES WITH CHICKEN AND VEGETABLES

4 oz/115 g cellophane noodles

1 tsp Asian sesame oil

CHICKEN AND SAUCE

12 oz/340 g skinless, boneless chicken breast halves

3 Tbsp soy sauce

1 tsp Asian sesame oil

2 tsp sugar

1 tsp sesame seeds

2 Tbsp plus 1 tsp vegetable oil

6 oz/170 g spinach leaves, stemmed and rinsed, but not dried

3 carrots, peeled and cut into julienne

6 large shiitake mushrooms, stemmed, caps thinly sliced

1 small yellow onion, cut into thin half-moons

6 green onions, white and green parts, chopped

3 garlic cloves, minced

1. Soak the cellophane noodles in a large bowl of hot water until softened and pliable, about 15 minutes. Do not let them soak until they are mushy. Drain in a sieve. Toss with the sesame oil in a medium bowl.

2. To marinate the chicken: Cut the chicken into crosswise slices about ¼ in/6 mm thick, then cut these into pieces about 2 in/5 cm long. Put in a medium bowl and toss with 1 Tbsp of the soy sauce and the sesame oil. Mix the remaining 2 Tbsp soy sauce with the sugar in a small bowl. Let both mixtures stand for about 15 minutes.

3. Heat a wok or large skillet over medium-high heat. Add the sesame seeds and cook, stirring often, until toasted, about 1 minute. Transfer to a platter. Add the 1 tsp oil to the wok and heat until hot but not smoking. Add the spinach and cook, stirring often, until tender, about 3 minutes. Drain in a sieve, pressing with the back of a large spoon to extract excess moisture. Coarsely chop the spinach.

4. Add 1 Tbsp of the oil to the wok. Add the marinated chicken and cook, stirring often, until it is just opaque, about 3 minutes. Transfer to a platter.

5. Add the remaining 1 Tbsp oil to the wok and heat. Add the carrots and mushrooms and stir until beginning to soften, about 1½ minutes. Add the onions and garlic and stir until the onions wilt, about 1 minute. Return the chicken to the wok and mix well. Add the noodles with the spinach and the soy mixture, stir well, and cook just until the noodles are hot, about 1 minute. Transfer to the platter, sprinkle with the sesame seeds, and serve.

MAKES 6 SERVINGS

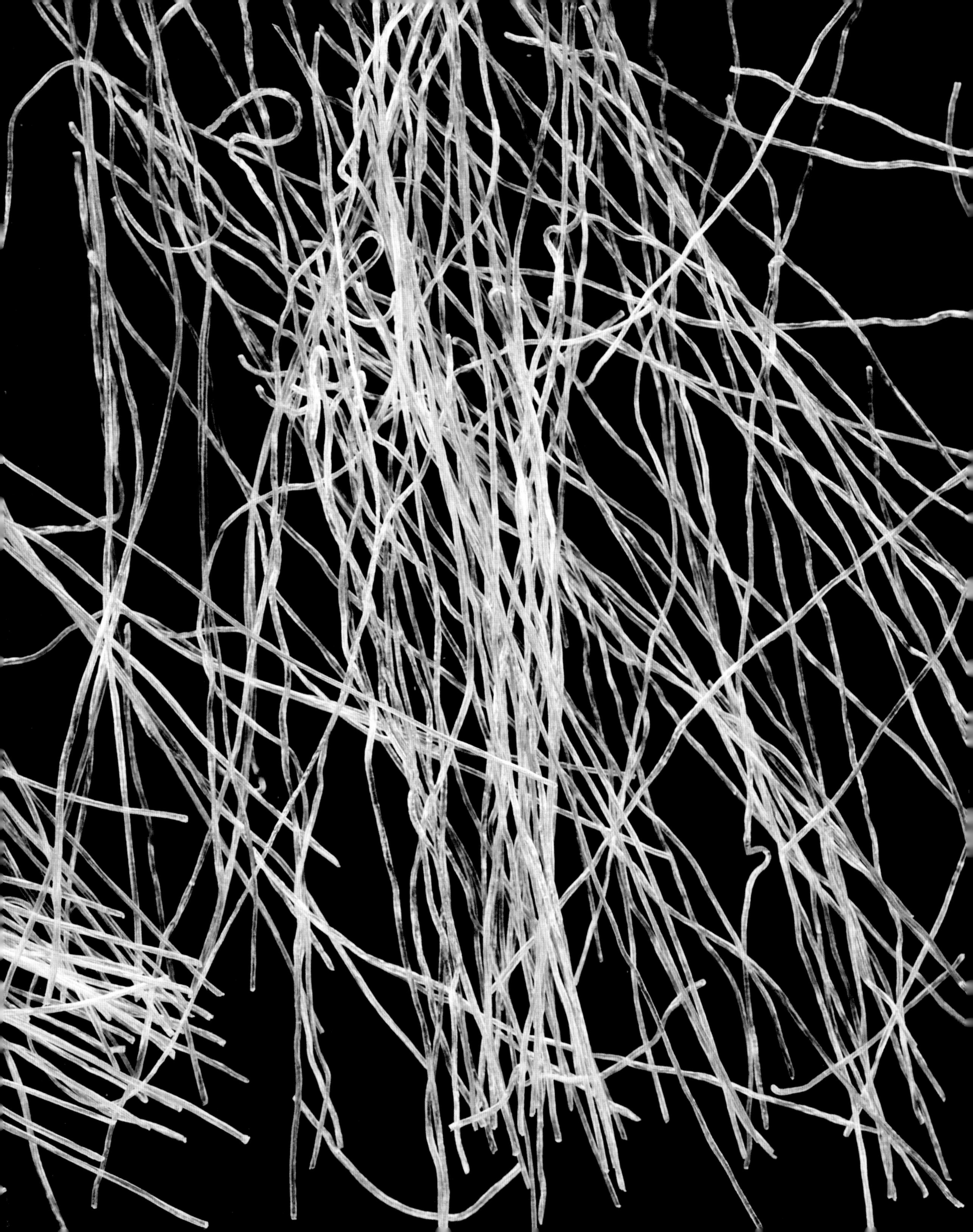

Dried hibiscus flowers (labeled *jamaica* in Latino markets) make a tart, magenta-colored beverage. Here, we use them to make a syrup to flavor and color this thirst-quencher of a cocktail. It is one of the few tropical drinks made with vodka. Because of vodka's popularity, you might want to make this your home bar's signature drink, and keep a jar of the syrup on hand.

HIBISCUS LIME COOLER

HIBISCUS SYRUP

½ cup/100 g sugar

⅓ cup/15 g dried hibiscus flowers (*jamaica*)

COCKTAIL

1½ fl oz/45 ml vodka

1 fl oz/30 ml Hibiscus Syrup, above

1 fl oz/30 ml fresh lime juice

1 fl oz/30 ml pineapple juice

½ fl oz/15 ml triple sec or Cointreau

GARNISH: Fresh mint sprig

1 **To make the syrup:** Bring the sugar and ½ cup/120 ml water to a boil in a small saucepan over high heat, stirring to dissolve the sugar. Remove from the heat and add the hibiscus flowers. Let stand for 15 minutes. Strain the syrup into a jar, pressing hard on the solids before discarding them. Let cool. (The syrup can be covered and refrigerated for up to 1 week.)

2 Add the cocktail ingredients to an ice-filled cocktail shaker. Shake well.

3 Fill a tall Collins glass with ice. Strain the cocktail into the glass. Garnish with the mint and serve.

MAKES 1 DRINK

Vodka didn't become popular in the United States until the 1960s, and up until then, most drinks were built with domestically made gin, bourbon, and rye. The latter is experiencing a comeback, and this drink gives it a tropical flair. Whiskey lovers don't see many cocktails for them in the tiki world, but this drink is a glorious exception.

HIBISCUS FIZZ

1½ fl oz/45 ml rye whiskey, such as Old Overholt

¾ fl oz/22.5 ml Simple Syrup (page 29)

¾ fl oz/22.5 ml Hibiscus Syrup, above

¼ fl oz/7.5 ml fresh lemon juice

1 large egg white (see Note)

Splash of club soda

GARNISH: Strip of orange zest

1 Fill a champagne coupe glass with ice cubes and set aside to chill. Shake the first five ingredients without ice in a cocktail shaker until foamy. Add ice cubes and shake well.

2 Empty the ice from the glass. Strain the cocktail into the chilled glass. Add a splash of soda, taking care not to disturb the foamy top. Garnish with the orange zest and serve.

MAKES 1 DRINK

NOTE: The consumption of raw or undercooked eggs may increase your risk of food-borne illness. To avoid using raw egg, substitute 2 Tbsp repasteurized egg white, available in the refrigerated section of the supermarket. Or, use an equal amount of reconstituted dried egg whites or meringue powder.

When it comes to homemade fried rice, cold rice is the only way to go, as freshly cooked rice quickly turns mushy when fried. Many Hawaiians habitually keep leftover rice to make a quick meal like this Korean version with kimchi, bacon, and peas. The meat could be ham or even Spam, with asparagus serving as the green vegetable.

FRIED RICE WITH KIMCHI, BACON, AND PEAS

6 slices bacon, cut into 1-in/2.5-cm pieces

2 Tbsp vegetable oil

2 celery stalks, thinly sliced

2 green onions, white and dark green parts separated and thinly sliced

2 garlic cloves, minced

1½ cups/400 g chopped Homemade Kimchi (page 158) with juices or purchased kimchi

3 cups/450 g cold cooked Hawaiian-Style Rice (page 157), made with long-grain rice

1 cup/155 g thawed frozen peas

2 tsp Asian sesame oil

1 Heat a large skillet over medium heat. Add the bacon and cook, stirring occasionally, until crisp and browned, 6 to 8 minutes. Using a slotted spoon, transfer the bacon to paper towels to drain. Pour out the fat and wipe out the skillet.

2 Add the oil to the skillet and heat over medium-high heat. Add the celery, white and pale green onion parts, and garlic and stir until the garlic is fragrant, about 30 seconds. Stir in the kimchi with its juices and cook until heated through, about 1 minute.

3 Stir in the rice and cook, stirring almost constantly and breaking up any clumps with the spoon, until the rice is hot, 3 to 4 minutes. During the last minute, stir in the peas.

4 Transfer to a platter. Sprinkle with the bacon and green onion leaves, drizzle with the sesame oil, and serve.

MAKES 4 TO 6 SERVINGS

Filipinos are the largest ethnic group in Hawaii, where their cuisine is based in home cooking, without a big restaurant presence. There are many treasured dishes worth adopting, including this fried rice with a crispy garlic topping. It is often enjoyed for breakfast with the meat and eggs on the side, but here they're added to the rice to make a more substantial lunch or supper dish.

GARLIC FRIED RICE WITH SAUSAGE, EGGS, AND GREEN ONIONS

2 Tbsp plus 2 tsp vegetable oil

4 large eggs

Pinch of kosher salt

8 garlic cloves, finely chopped (but not minced)

2½ oz/70 g Chinese sausage or smoked chorizo, cut into small dice

4 cups/600 g cold cooked Hawaiian-Style Rice (page 157), made with long-grain rice)

2 green onions, white and green parts, thinly sliced

1 Tbsp soy sauce

1 Heat the 2 tsp oil in a medium nonstick skillet over medium heat. Beat the eggs and salt together in a medium bowl. Pour into the skillet and cook, lifting up the edges of the cooked eggs as they set with a heat-proof spatula and tilting the pan so the uncooked portion flows underneath, just until the omelet is set, about 2 minutes. Cover the skillet, reduce the heat to low, and cook until the top is set, about 1 minute more. Slide the omelet out of the skillet onto a plate. Let cool. Cut the omelet in half, and then into strips about ½ in/12 mm wide.

2 Heat the 2 Tbsp oil in a wok or large skillet over medium heat until it is hot and shimmering. Add the garlic and stir until it is crisp and golden brown, about 30 seconds. Using a slotted spoon, transfer the garlic to a small bowl, leaving the oil in the wok. Be sure to remove all the bits of garlic from the wok.

3 Add the sausage and cook, stirring often, until it begins to brown, about 1 minute. Increase the heat to high. Stir in the rice and cook, stirring almost constantly and breaking up clumps with the spoon, until the rice is hot, 3 to 4 minutes. During the last minute, stir in the green onions and soy sauce.

4 Spoon the rice into individual bowls and top with the garlic and omelet strips. Serve hot.

MAKES 4 SERVINGS

Chow mein is an American invention that borrowed from several different Chinese dishes. It has long been a staple of Honolulu's Chinatown restaurants, along with other mild Cantonese-style dishes. Today, it remains delicious, comforting, and fun to make, with a crisp, thick disk of fried noodles acting as a bed for a saucy stir-fry. Use your favorite vegetables in this recipe, and add a sprinkle of red pepper flakes, if you like.

CHINATOWN CHOW MEIN WITH PORK AND MUSHROOMS

NOODLE CAKE

6 oz/170 g lo mein (Chinese egg noodles) or spaghetti

1 Tbsp plus ⅔ cup/165 ml vegetable oil, plus more as needed

STIR-FRY

1¼ cups/300 ml canned reduced-sodium beef broth

3 Tbsp soy sauce

1 Tbsp molasses

¼ tsp freshly ground black pepper

1 Tbsp cornstarch

3 Tbsp vegetable oil

1 lb/455 g boneless country-style pork ribs, cut into 1-in/2.5-cm pieces

1 large yellow onion, cut into thin half-moons

8 oz/225 g white button mushrooms, thinly sliced

3 large celery stalks, cut into diagonal slices about ¼ in/6 mm thick

2 cups/140 g fresh bean sprouts

1 To make the noodle cake: Bring a large pot of salted water to a boil over high heat. Add the noodles and cook according to the package instructions until tender. Drain and rinse under cold running water. Drain well. Drizzle with the 1 Tbsp oil and toss well.

2 Position a rack in the center of the oven and preheat the oven to 200°F/100°C. Heat a large wok or skillet over medium-high heat. Line a large rimmed baking sheet with brown paper or paper towels.

3 Add the ⅔ cup/165 ml oil and heat until shimmering. Carefully add the noodles and spread them into a thick cake. Cook until the underside is golden brown, 3 to 4 minutes. Using two wooden spoons, carefully flip the noodles in the pan and continue cooking until the other side is crisp and golden brown, about 4 minutes more. Transfer the noodle cake to the baking sheet and keep warm in the oven while making the stir-fry. Pour out the oil in the pan.

4 To make the stir-fry: Mix the broth, soy sauce, molasses, and pepper together in a medium bowl. Sprinkle in the cornstarch and stir to dissolve the cornstarch.

5 Heat the skillet or wok over medium-high heat until hot. Add 1 Tbsp of the oil and heat until it is very hot but not smoking. Add the pork and cook, stirring often, until it is browned and shows no sign of pink when pierced in the center with the tip of a knife, about 5 minutes. Transfer to a platter.

6 Add the remaining 2 Tbsp oil to the skillet and heat until it is very hot but not smoking. Add the onion, mushrooms, and celery and cook, stirring often, until the celery is crisp-tender, about 3 minutes. Return the pork and any juices on the platter to the skillet. Stir the broth mixture to blend in the cornstarch, stir it into the pan, and bring to a boil. Add the bean sprouts and mix just until they are heated through and the sauce has thickened, about 1 minute. Remove from the heat.

7 Transfer the noodle cake to a round serving platter. Top with the stir-fry and serve.

MAKES 4 SERVINGS

Pho (pronounced "fuh"), a classic Vietnamese beef and noodle soup, features a deeply flavored and gently spiced stock that is always made from scratch. Cooks can choose from a variety of beef cuts, including using beef tendon or ground meatballs in this dish; here we use thinly sliced rib roast, accompanied with traditional garnishes. All of these components can and should be prepared well ahead of serving so the final cooking takes only a few minutes.

VIETNAMESE NOODLE SOUP WITH BEEF

STOCK

1½ lb/680 g beef marrow bones

1½ lb/680 g meaty beef bones, such as neck or chuck

1 yellow onion, coarsely chopped

One 1-in/2.5-cm piece fresh ginger, peeled and thinly sliced

1 tsp whole coriander seeds

3 star anise pods

¼ tsp whole cloves

3 Tbsp Thai or Vietnamese fish sauce

2 Tbsp light brown sugar

1½ lb/680 g boneless rib roast

14 oz/400 g dried thin rice noodles

2 cups/140 g fresh bean sprouts

Leaves from 4 large sprigs fresh Thai basil

Leaves from 4 large sprigs fresh cilantro

2 green onions, white and green parts, thinly sliced

2 small fresh red or green chiles, such as Thai, thinly sliced with seeds

1 lime, cut into wedges

Fish sauce, for serving

Hoisin sauce, for serving

1 Put both kinds of bones in a large stockpot and add cold water to just cover the bones. Bring to a boil over high heat. Drain and rinse the bones under cold running water. (This step removes many of the impurities that would cloud the stock, and a clear stock is one sign of a good pho.) Clean the pot.

2 Return the bones to the pot and add cold water to cover the bones by 2 in/5 cm. Bring to a boil over high heat, skimming off any foam that rises to the surface. Add the onion, ginger, coriander, star anise, and cloves. Reduce the heat to low and simmer, skimming as needed until the stock is full flavored, at least 2 or up to 4 hours. During the last few minutes, stir in the fish sauce and brown sugar. Strain through a colander into a large bowl and discard the solids. Return 6 cups/1.4 L stock to the pot. (Do not remove any fat from the surface, as this adds flavor to the stock.) Reserve the remaining stock for another use. (The stock can be cooled, covered, and refrigerated for up to 2 days or frozen for up to 3 months.)

3 Meanwhile, freeze the beef until partially frozen, about 2 hours. Using a sharp, thin knife, cut the beef crosswise into very thin slices. Let stand at room temperature to defrost, up to 30 minutes.

4 Put the rice noodles in a large bowl and add hot water to cover. Let stand until the noodles are softened but not mushy, about 15 minutes.

5 Meanwhile, arrange the bean sprouts, basil and cilantro leaves, green onions, chiles, and lime wedges on a large platter (or in 4 individual bowls) for garnishing and flavoring the pho.

6 Drain the noodles. Immediately divide the noodles among 4 large, deep Asian-style soup bowls. Divide the beef slices among the bowls. Ladle in equal amounts of the hot stock. Serve immediately with the platter (or bowls) of flavorings, as well as the fish sauce and hoisin sauce for seasoning.

MAKES 4 SERVINGS

Pancit simply means "noodle" in Filipino, but this recipe uses *pancit canton*, curly yellow flour noodles. Cooked in the broth rather than being boiled separately, the noodles take on a toothsome texture and deep flavor. The shrimp and chorizo show the Spanish influence on Filipino cooking.

PAN-COOKED NOODLES WITH SHRIMP AND CHORIZO (*PANCIT*)

2 Tbsp vegetable oil

5 oz/140 g smoked chorizo, cut into ½-in/12-mm dice

8 oz/225 g large (31 to 35 count) shrimp, peeled and deveined

2 cups/200 g chopped green cabbage

1 yellow onion, cut into thin half-moons

1 large carrot, peeled and julienned on a V-slicer or mandoline (or cut with a knife)

½ large red bell pepper, seeded, deribbed, and julienned

2 garlic cloves, finely chopped

1 cup /85 g bias-cut snow peas, cut about ½ in/12 mm wide

4 cups/960 ml Asian Chicken Broth (page 149) or canned reduced-sodium chicken broth

¼ cup/60 ml soy sauce

2 Tbsp oyster sauce

1½ packages *pancit canton* (Filipino flour noodles), about 12 oz/340 g total

Lime wedges, for serving

1 Heat 1 Tbsp of the oil in a large wok or deep, heavy skillet over medium heat. Add the chorizo and cook, stirring occasionally, until beginning to brown, about 1 minute. Add the shrimp and cook, stirring occasionally, until they turn pink and opaque, 2 to 3 minutes. Transfer the mixture to a platter.

2 Add the remaining 1 Tbsp oil to the wok and heat until hot but not smoking. Add the cabbage, onion, carrot, bell pepper, and garlic and cook, stirring often, until the vegetables are crisp-tender, about 4 minutes. During the last minute, stir in the snow peas to heat them. Transfer the vegetables to the platter.

3 Add the broth, soy sauce, and oyster sauce to the wok and bring the mixture to a boil over high heat, scraping up any browned bits in the wok with a wooden spoon. Stack two *pancit* noodle layers on top of each other in the wok. Let the noodles cook until the bottom layer softens in the broth mixture, about 30 seconds. Using two wooden spoons, toss the noodles in the wok until softened, about 1 minute. Add the remaining noodles and toss them until softened, about 1 minute. Reduce the heat to medium and boil, tossing almost constantly, until the noodles are just tender, 8 to 10 minutes. Return the vegetables, shrimp, and chorizo to the wok and toss until combined.

4 Transfer the *pancit* to a platter. Add the limes and serve.

MAKES 6 SERVINGS

Saimin, a noodle soup that can seem to contain almost everything but the kitchen sink, is possibly Hawaii's most popular food (even McDonald's was convinced to add it to their Islands menu). This jumble of Asian noodle dishes is commonly sold at the many food stands that dot the Islands. While some saimin broths have a seaweed base, this one uses chicken broth. Prepare using the Braised Pork Belly on page 92, or use a topping of your choice.

SAIMIN WITH ASIAN CHICKEN BROTH

ASIAN CHICKEN BROTH

3 lb/1.4 kg chicken wings

2 green onions, coarsely chopped

4 quarter-sized slices fresh ginger, coarsely chopped

3 garlic cloves, crushed with flat side of a knife

½ tsp black peppercorns

Kosher salt

THIN SOUP OMELETS

2 large eggs

Pinch of kosher salt

1 tsp vegetable oil

1 lb/455 g fresh saimin noodles (see Glossary, page 213)

8 oz/225 g sliced Braised Pork (page 92), about ½ recipe

16 slices *kamaboko* (Japanese fish cake), cut ¼ in/6 mm thick

2 green onions, white and green parts, thinly sliced

Soy sauce, for serving

1 To make the broth: Combine the wings, green onions, ginger, and garlic in a large stockpot and add cold water to cover by 1 in/2.5 cm. Bring to a boil over high heat, skimming off the foam that rises to the surface. Add the peppercorns. Reduce the heat to low and simmer uncovered until full flavored, at least 2 or up to 4 hours. Season to taste with salt. Strain through a colander into a large bowl and discard the solids. Return 6 cups/1.4 L of broth to the pot and keep hot over low heat. (Do not remove any fat from the surface, as this adds flavor to the broth.) Reserve the remaining broth for another use. (The broth can be cooled, covered, and refrigerated for up to 2 days or frozen for up to 3 months.)

2 To make the omelets: Whisk the eggs together in a medium bowl with a pinch of salt. Heat ½ tsp of the oil in a small nonstick skillet over medium heat. Add half of the egg mixture and cook, lifting up the edges of the cooked eggs as they set with a heat-proof spatula and tilting the pan so the uncooked portion flows underneath, just until the omelet is set and has a shiny top, about 1½ minutes. Using the spatula, roll up the omelet and transfer to a plate. Repeat with the remaining egg mixture and oil. Stack, roll, and cut the omelets crosswise into thin strips.

3 Bring a large pot of salted water to a boil over high heat. Add the noodles and cook according to the package directions. Drain the noodles in a colander and rinse under warm water.

4 Immediately divide the noodles among 4 large, deep Asian-style soup bowls. Add equal amounts of the hot broth to each bowl. Top each with equal amounts of the pork, *kamaboko*, green onions, and omelet strips. Serve hot, with the soy sauce for seasoning.

MAKES 4 SERVINGS

Saimin Toppings

Here are some other suggestions for topping your saimin:

- Cubed ham or Spam
- Shredded Kalua Pork (page 99)
- Cooked strips of chicken breast
- Cooked shrimp
- Cooked green peas
- Shredded napa cabbage
- Thinly sliced bok choy
- Julienned carrots
- Soaked and sliced dried shiitake mushrooms
- Enoki mushrooms
- Fried or scrambled eggs

Most mainland cooks know ramen as inexpensive blocks of Japanese curly thin noodles, but fresh ramen is a true delicacy that deserves a carefully prepared broth. Soy sauce (called by its Japanese name, *shoyu*, in Hawaii) is one of the four main ramen broth seasonings (the others being salt, miso, and boiled pork bones).

PORK RAMEN WITH SHOYU BROTH

BROTH

2 lb/910 g chicken wings, chopped between joints and rinsed under cold water

1 lb/455 g pork spareribs

6 green onions, white and green parts, coarsely chopped

One 2-in/5-cm piece fresh ginger, thinly sliced

4 garlic cloves

½ tsp black peppercorns

3 large eggs

1½ lb/680 g boneless country-style pork ribs

SEASONING

3 Tbsp soy sauce

3 Tbsp good-quality sake, such as Gekkeikan Traditional

1 lb/455 g fresh ramen noodles or linguine (see Note)

One 8-oz/225-g can bamboo shoots, drained and cut into thin strips

16 slices *kamaboko* (Japanese fish cake)

2 sheets toasted nori, each cut into thirds to make 6 strips

1 To make the broth: Combine the wings, spareribs, green onions, ginger, and garlic in a large stockpot and add cold water to cover by 2 in/5 cm. Bring to a boil over high heat, skimming off the foam that rises to the surface. Add the peppercorns. Reduce the heat to low and simmer, skimming as needed, until full flavored, at least 2 or up to 4 hours. Strain through a colander into a large bowl and discard the solids. Return 8 cups/2 L broth to the pot. (Do not remove any fat from the surface, as this adds flavor to the broth.) Reserve the remaining broth for another use. (The broth can be cooled, covered, and refrigerated for up to 2 days or frozen for up to 3 months.)

2 Meanwhile, soft boil the eggs: Using a pin, prick a hole in the wider end of each egg, just piercing the shell and not reaching the inner egg. Place the eggs in a small saucepan and add water to cover. Bring to a boil over medium heat. Reduce the heat to medium-low and simmer for 7 minutes exactly. Using a slotted spoon, transfer the eggs to ice water and let stand until chilled, at least 10 minutes. Carefully peel the eggs—they will have a jelly-like texture. Refrigerate until ready to serve.

3 Return the broth to a simmer over medium-low heat. Add the boneless pork ribs to the simmering broth and cook until tender, about 30 minutes. Remove the pork from the broth and transfer to a cutting board. Let stand for 5 minutes. Cut the ribs crosswise into wide, thin slices. Transfer to a bowl. (The pork can cool slightly.) Cut each egg in half lengthwise.

4 To make the seasoning: Mix the ingredients together in a small bowl.

5 Meanwhile, bring a large pot of water to a boil. Add the noodles and cook according to the package directions. Drain the noodles in a colander and rinse under warm water.

6 Spoon 1 Tbsp of the seasoning into each of 6 large, deep Asian-style soup bowls. Divide the noodles, followed by the broth, among the soup bowls. Top each with equal amounts of the sliced pork, bamboo shoots, and *kamaboko*. Add an egg half and nori strip to each bowl and serve immediately.

MAKES 6 SERVINGS

NOTE: Fresh ramen noodles are available at Asian markets. Truthfully, as long as you have a full-flavored broth, almost any good fresh or dried noodle works here, including dried udon and even cheap ramen—as long as you skip the powdered soup base.

Steve Sakala's personal voyage mirrors the travels of European sailors who settled in the Hawaiian Islands some 150 years ago. Steve grew up in Southern California and watched the neighboring citrus orchards being paved over for parking lots. Looking for unspoiled nature, he moved north to the California redwood forests, where he earned a bachelor of science in natural resources and city planning at Humboldt State University. But a subsequent four-year stint in West Africa with the Peace Corps is what set Steve on his current quest.

"In Africa, I learned how community and agriculture are interconnected," he says. Back home in California, a chance encounter led him to a group of people who were building a retreat in Hawaii. They asked Steve for help developing an agricultural model. "I worked with them for a year," Steve recalls.

Then, a more personal vision inspired Steve to create the exquisite 7½-acre mountaintop community called Honaunau EcoRetreat and Farm. "It's a multifaceted place, where living is on multiple levels," he explains. This includes organic fruit and vegetable farming as well as raising goats and sheep for milk. The property is also home to chickens and ducks. "Sixty to seventy percent of our meals come from the farm," Steve notes with pride. Additional farm produce is sold to local markets and restaurants.

But it is the spiritual component that distinguishes Honaunau from many agricultural endeavors. "What we do here allows us to reconnect to the land and to ourselves," Steve notes. For this farmer-philosopher and the ten people who work or live there, the farm is a place where "we acknowledge divine design by growing things."

Honaunau also offers intimate classes in such holistic pursuits as tai chi and yoga, along with therapeutic perks such as saunas and massage for those staying in the retreat's guest house.

"We're looking for a balance between work and play," Steve says. "And we strive to create a new model that brings a more holistic approach to living."

HONAUNAU FARM, HONAUNAU-NAPOOPOO

SIDE DISHES AND BREADS

The most important side dish in Hawaiian cooking is rice, as it accompanies so many of the favorite main courses that feature savory sauces and gravies. Stir-fried vegetables are a favorite choice to serve alongside meats, poultry, and seafood. And Portuguese rolls and skillet-cooked Indian flatbread are essential companions for many Island meals.

157 HAWAIIAN-STYLE RICE

158 CABBAGE AND DAIKON KIMCHI

160 DRUNKEN MUSHROOMS

161 WASABI–ROASTED GARLIC MASHED POTATOES

162 BRAISED BABY BOK CHOY WITH MACADAMIA NUTS

165 SESAME AND GINGER SPINACH

168 ASPARAGUS WITH OYSTER SAUCE

169 GREEN ONION AND GARLIC NAAN

170 BROCCOLINI WITH CHILE–LEMON OIL

172 EGGPLANT IN BLACK BEAN SAUCE

175 GREEN TEA RICE WITH PEAS

176 PORTUGUESE SWEET BREAD ROLLS

Hawaiian households serve rice for at least two (and sometimes three) meals a day. Some cultures prefer medium-grain rice because it's easier to pick up with chopsticks, while others like the fluffier texture of long grain. Most Hawaiians use a rice cooker, but the stove-top method works for either rice variety and can be multiplied for more servings—the depth of water needed to cook the rice will stay the same.

HAWAIIAN-STYLE RICE

1 cup/215 g medium-grain (such as Calrose) or long-grain rice (such as Carolina, basmati, or jasmine)

½ tsp kosher salt (optional)

1 Whether you rinse the rice or not is a matter of choice. If you rinse it, the grains will be slightly less sticky, but you will also be rinsing away the vitamins that are sprayed on after processing away the bran. If you do rinse, put the rice in a sieve and rinse it well under cold running water, moving the rice around with one hand while the other holds the sieve, until the water looks clear.

2 To avoid boiling over, choose a small, heavy saucepan that will hold the expanded rice with at least 1 in/2.5 cm of headroom—raw rice triples in volume during cooking. Put your fingertip on top of the rice, then add enough cold water to reach your first knuckle (about 1 in/2.5 cm). Bring the water to a boil over high heat. Add the salt, if using. (Most Hawaiians do not salt the rice, because the sauce on the main course is usually flavored with soy sauce or another salty ingredient.)

3 Reduce the heat to medium-low and tightly cover the saucepan. Cook at a steady simmer, without stirring, until the rice has absorbed the liquid and is tender. Remove from the heat and let stand, covered, for 5 minutes. This gives the rice a chance to absorb any remaining liquid and settle a bit. It will stay warm, covered, for 15 to 20 minutes. (Rice is always best served soon after cooking. However, leftover rice can be cooled, covered, and refrigerated for up to 2 days to use for fried rice.)

MAKES 4 SERVINGS

You can buy kimchi at Asian markets, but it is easy and fun to make at home. This recipe for the classic mix of cabbage and daikon makes a relatively small amount. (Many Hawaiian cooks make kimchi by the barrel.) The kimchi will continue to ferment and take on a more sour flavor in the refrigerator, so use it within a month.

CABBAGE AND DAIKON KIMCHI

½ head napa cabbage, about 1 lb/455 g

1 lb/455 g daikon (white radish), peeled

2 Tbsp kosher salt

6 green onions, white and green parts, thinly sliced into rounds

¼ cup/60 ml Thai or Vietnamese fish sauce

¼ cup/30 g *gochugaru* (Korean chili flakes); see Notes

¼ cup/40 g peeled and minced fresh ginger

6 large garlic cloves, minced

1 tsp sugar

SPECIAL EQUIPMENT: One 8-cup/2-L glass canning jar (see Notes)

1 Cut the cabbage in half lengthwise and cut out the core. Cut the cabbage coarsely into pieces about 2 in/5 cm square. Cut the daikon into thin strips about 2 in/5 cm long and ⅛ in/3 mm wide. (Use a knife for this so the strips aren't too thin.) Transfer to a bowl, sprinkle with the salt, and mix well with your hands to separate the cabbage leaves. Let stand for 2 hours. Rinse very well and drain.

2 A handful at a time, squeeze the excess liquid from the cabbage and transfer the cabbage and daikon to a large bowl. Add the green onions, fish sauce, chili flakes, ginger, garlic, and sugar and mix with long tongs. (Do not use your hands, unless you wear latex gloves.)

3 Have a clean 8-cup/2-L glass canning jar ready. Using the tongs, transfer the cabbage mixture to the hot jar. Using a long wooden spoon, crush the mixture in the jar to release enough juices to barely cover the vegetables. Cover the jar with its lid. Let stand at room temperature, opening the jar every 8 hours or so to release the building gases, until you see bubbles forming in the juices in the jar, 12 to 36 hours, depending on the ambient temperature. The warmer the temperature, the quicker fermentation will occur.

4 Transfer the kimchi to a 4-cup/960-ml covered container (it doesn't have to be glass at this point). Refrigerate for up to 1 month.

MAKES 4 CUPS/910 G KIMCHI

NOTES: Korean chili flakes (*gochugaru*), essential for making kimchi, are available at Asian markets and online. Korean chili powder is not the same, as it is more finely ground and spicier than the flakes. You can use leftover Korean chili flakes as an all-purpose seasoning, similar to but milder than cayenne. If you can't find Korean chili flakes, substitute 2 Tbsp Hungarian paprika and 2 Tbsp red pepper flakes.

Follow the manufacturer's instructions for safely preheating the canning jar and lid before using.

If you are looking for a side dish to go with grilled steaks, try this mushroom sauté, which is soused with a good dose of sake. While you could use only one kind of mushroom, a variety gives the dish visual interest and ratchets the flavor up a notch, too. A trip to an Asian market will reveal a huge array of fungi of many sizes.

DRUNKEN MUSHROOMS

1¼ lb/570 g assorted mushrooms, such as shiitakes, oyster mushrooms, enoki, and king mushrooms

1 Tbsp vegetable oil

2 green onions, white and pale green parts finely chopped, dark green leaves thinly sliced

2 garlic cloves, minced

¼ cup/60 ml canned reduced-sodium chicken broth

¼ cup/60 ml sake

1 Tbsp soy sauce

1 tsp cornstarch

1 Prepare the mushrooms, cutting them into pieces about the same size so they cook at the same rate: For shiitake mushrooms, cut off and discard the stems and cut the caps into ½-in/12-mm strips. Oyster mushrooms should be cut lengthwise into pieces about ½ in/12 mm thick. Cut the clump of enoki mushrooms lengthwise into sections with a few mushrooms each. Cut king mushrooms crosswise into rounds about ½ in/12 mm thick.

2 Heat a wok or large skillet over medium-high heat. Add the oil and heat until very hot but not smoking. Add the white and pale green onion parts and garlic and stir until the garlic is fragrant, about 30 seconds. Add the mushrooms and cook, stirring occasionally, until tender, about 5 minutes.

3 Mix the broth, sake, and soy sauce together in a small bowl. Stir in the cornstarch. Stir the broth mixture into the mushrooms and reduce the heat to medium-low. Cook until the broth mixture comes to a simmer and thickens, about 1 minute. Transfer to a serving bowl. Sprinkle with the green onion leaves and serve.

MAKES 4 SERVINGS

The New Hawaiian Cuisine movement innovated wasabi mashed potatoes, which transformed an old standard with exciting new flavors. Here is our take on this dish, with roasted garlic for even more oomph. Try it with a meaty fish, such as swordfish or salmon. An electric mixer does fast work of whipping the potatoes into smooth mounds, but you can use a ricer or masher, too. (Do not use a food processor, or you will end up with *mushed* potatoes.)

WASABI–ROASTED GARLIC MASHED POTATOES

ROASTED GARLIC

1 large head garlic

⅓ cup/75 ml olive oil, or as needed

3 lb/1.4 kg baking potatoes, peeled and cut into 1½-in/4-cm chunks

2 Tbsp wasabi powder

½ tsp cider vinegar

4 Tbsp/55 g unsalted butter, at room temperature

⅓ cup/75 ml heavy cream, warmed, as needed

Kosher salt and freshly ground black pepper

1 To roast the garlic: Position a rack in the center of the oven and preheat the oven to 350°F/180°C. Break the garlic head into cloves. Lightly smash each clove with the flat side of a large knife and peel the cloves. Transfer the garlic cloves to a custard cup and add enough oil to cover them. Bake until the garlic is golden brown and tender, about 40 minutes. Remove from the oven and let stand for 30 minutes. Drain the garlic, reserving the oil for another dish. Using a fork, mash the garlic into a coarse purée, then set aside. (The garlic can be covered and refrigerated for up to 3 days. Bring to room temperature before using.)

2 Put the potatoes in a large saucepan and add salted cold water to cover. Cover and bring to a boil over high heat. Reduce the heat to medium-low and set the lid ajar. Simmer until the potatoes are tender when pierced with the tip of a sharp knife, 25 to 30 minutes.

3 Just before the potatoes are done, stir the wasabi powder, 2 Tbsp boiling water, and the vinegar together in a small bowl to make a paste.

4 Drain the potatoes well. Return them to the saucepan and cook over low heat, stirring often, until they begin to film the bottom of the pot, about 2 minutes. Remove from the heat.

5 Add the butter, roasted garlic, and wasabi paste to the potatoes. Beat with a hand-held electric mixer on medium speed, adding the warmed cream as needed for the desired consistency, until the potatoes are smooth. Season to taste with salt and pepper. Transfer to a warmed serving bowl and serve immediately.

MAKES 6 SERVINGS

Despite its name, baby bok choy is not an immature version of the standard supermarket variety. Asian markets label it Shanghai bok choy, its actual name. These little guys are sweeter and less bitter than their big cousins, and the whole ones look jaunty on the plate. Here's a recipe that gives them a tender texture with a crunchy accent from macadamia nuts.

BRAISED BABY BOK CHOY WITH MACADAMIA NUTS

4 baby (Shanghai) bok choy, about 1 lb/455 g

1 Tbsp vegetable oil

2 tsp peeled and finely minced fresh ginger

2 garlic cloves, minced

½ small fresh hot red chile, thinly sliced with seeds

½ cup/120 ml canned reduced-sodium chicken broth

1 Tbsp Thai or Vietnamese fish sauce or soy sauce

3 Tbsp coarsely chopped unsalted macadamia nuts

1 Rinse the baby bok choy well under cold running water, opening up the leaves to remove any grit but keeping the bok choy intact. Shake off the excess water.

2 Heat the oil in a large skillet over medium heat until very hot but not smoking. Add the ginger, garlic, and chile and stir until fragrant, about 15 seconds. Add the bok choy, then the broth and fish sauce and bring to a boil. Cover the skillet and reduce the heat to medium-low.

3 Simmer until the bok choy is just tender when pierced with the tip of a small, sharp knife, 12 to 15 minutes. Using a slotted spoon, transfer the bok choy to a serving bowl and tent with aluminum foil to keep warm.

4 Return the skillet to high heat and boil the cooking liquid until reduced by half, about 2 minutes. Pour the liquid over the bok choy. Sprinkle with the macadamia nuts and serve.

MAKES 4 SERVINGS

No doubt about it: bagged spinach is convenient. But try this recipe with bunch spinach, which has a more delicate texture, yet a deeper flavor, than the industrialized version. This recipe flavors the spinach with ginger, garlic, sesame seeds, and oil for an Asian-style side dish to serve with main courses. (And yes, you can make this with baby spinach.)

SESAME AND GINGER SPINACH

Leaves from 2 lb/910 g bunch spinach, stemmed

1½ tsp sesame seeds

1 Tbsp vegetable oil

1 Tbsp peeled and minced fresh ginger

2 garlic cloves, minced

Kosher salt

1 tsp Asian sesame oil

1 Fill a sink with cold water. Add the spinach and agitate it well to loosen any grit. Lift out the spinach, shaking off the excess water, and transfer it to large rimmed baking sheet, leaving the grit behind at the bottom of the sink. Repeat to be sure the spinach is clean. Do not dry the spinach.

2 Heat a large wok or skillet over medium-high heat. Add the sesame seeds and cook, stirring often, until toasted, about 1 minute. Transfer the seeds to a plate.

3 Add the oil to the skillet and heat until very hot but not smoking. Add the ginger and garlic and stir until fragrant, about 15 seconds. In batches, stir in the spinach, letting the first batch wilt before adding more. After all of the spinach has been added, cook just until the spinach is tender and hot, 1 to 2 minutes. Season to taste with salt. Transfer the spinach to a serving bowl, leaving any excess cooking liquid in the skillet. Sprinkle with the sesame seeds, drizzle with the sesame oil, and serve.

MAKES 4 TO 6 SERVINGS

The granddaddy of all tiki drinks, this long, tall gin-based libation was popularized in the early twentieth century at the Raffles Hotel in Singapore. Because Britain ruled so much of Asia at the time, gin was the preferred liquor, and vodka consumption was restricted to Russia. A Sling is just the thing to sip when riding in a rickshaw (after all, someone else is driving) or hanging out in a hammock on a hot day.

SINGAPORE SLING

2 fl oz/60 ml pineapple juice

1½ fl oz/45 ml London gin, such as Beefeater's

½ fl oz/15 ml cherry brandy, such as Cherry Heering

½ fl oz/15 ml Bénédictine

½ fl oz/15 ml fresh lime juice

½ fl oz/15 ml club soda

¼ fl oz/7.5 ml triple sec or Cointreau

¼ fl oz/7.5 ml grenadine

GARNISH: Large strip of orange zest, Marasca cherry

1 Add the ingredients to an ice-filled cocktail shaker. Stir well.

2 Fill a tall Collins glass with ice. Strain the cocktail into the glass. Spear the zest and cherry onto a wooden skewer. Garnish with the skewer and serve.

MAKES 1 DRINK

"Trader Vic" Bergeson's reputation as a master mixologist is based on this heady cocktail. Unlike the Caribbean Islands, Hawaii did not distill much of its sugarcane into rum, mostly because of the high cost of export. Bergeson simply used rum in his drink mainly because he needed to use up the overstock at his joint in Oakland, California.

MAI TAI

COCKTAIL

1 fl oz/30 ml white or silver rum, such as Bacardi

1 fl oz/30 ml triple sec or Cointreau

1 fl oz/30 ml orgeat syrup (see Note)

¾ fl oz/22.5 ml From-Scratch Sour Mix (recipe follows)

¾ fl oz/22.5 ml pineapple juice

½ fl oz/15 ml fresh lime juice

1 fl oz/30 ml dark rum, such as Myers's

FROM-SCRATCH SOUR MIX

½ cup/120 ml fresh orange juice

2 Tbsp/30 ml fresh lime or lemon juice (preferably 1 Tbsp/15 ml each)

¼ cup/50 g superfine sugar

GARNISH: Edible orchid

1 **To make the sour mix:** Shake the ingredients with ½ cup/120 ml water in a covered jar until the sugar is dissolved. (The mix can be refrigerated for up to 1 week.)

2 Add the cocktail ingredients to an ice-filled cocktail shaker. Shake well.

3 Fill a double old-fashioned glass with ice. Strain the cocktail into the glass. Garnish with the orchid and serve.

MAKES 1 DRINK

NOTE: Orgeat, a syrup flavored with almond and rose water, is available at well-stocked liquor stores. If necessary, substitute an equal amount of almond syrup (the kind used in Italian sodas and to flavor tea and coffee) with a drop of rose water.

A couple of tablespoons of oyster sauce (which must be one of the most flavor-packed ingredients on the planet) is the starting point for a simple side dish that could become a staple at your house. Although excellent with the asparagus in this recipe, it is easily adaptable to other vegetables. Try it with broccoli, broccolini, and baby (Shanghai) bok choy.

ASPARAGUS WITH OYSTER SAUCE

1 lb/455 g asparagus, trimmed and cut on a slight diagonal into pieces about ¾ in/2 cm long

2 Tbsp oyster sauce

2 Tbsp canned reduced-sodium chicken broth or water

1 Tbsp vegetable oil

3 garlic cloves, minced

1 tsp Asian sesame oil, for serving

2 Tbsp coarsely chopped unsalted dry-roasted peanuts or cashews (optional)

1 Pour ½-in/12-mm water into a large skillet and bring to a boil over high heat. Add the asparagus, cover, and cook until crisp-tender, about 3 minutes. Drain in a colander. Do not rinse the asparagus.

2 Wipe out the skillet. Stir the oyster sauce and broth together in a small bowl. Add the oil to the skillet and heat over medium-high heat until very hot but not smoking. Add the garlic and stir just until fragrant, about 15 seconds. Stir in the oyster sauce mixture and add the asparagus. Cook, tossing constantly, until the sauce mixture is boiling and has coated the asparagus, about 30 seconds. Transfer to a serving bowl. Drizzle with the sesame oil, sprinkle with the peanuts, if using, and serve.

MAKES 4 SERVINGS

Home ovens are not common in many Asian cultures, so flatbreads are often griddled over heat. This Indian flatbread is perfect for soaking up curry sauces, and can even be used as a wrap for other foods. While naan can be served at room temperature, they are best served right from the skillet.

GREEN ONION AND GARLIC NAAN

DOUGH

½ tsp active dry yeast

¾ cup/180 ml warm (about 110°F/43°C) water

¼ cup/60 ml plain Greek yogurt

3 Tbsp unsalted butter, melted

3 cups/420 g unbleached all-purpose flour

2 Tbsp sugar

1¼ tsp fine sea salt

1 tsp baking powder

½ tsp baking soda

5 Tbsp/70 g unsalted butter

2 green onions, white and green parts, minced

2 garlic cloves, minced

1 To make the dough: Sprinkle the yeast over ¼ cup/60 ml of the warm water in a medium bowl. Let stand for 5 minutes, then stir to dissolve the yeast. Stir in the remaining ½ cup/120 ml warm water with the yogurt and melted butter.

2 Using a whisk, stir the flour, sugar, salt, baking powder, and baking soda together in the bowl of a stand mixer or a large bowl. Make a well in the center and pour in the yeast mixture. Using a stand mixer fitted with the paddle attachment, mix on low speed to make a soft dough that barely clears the side of the bowl, adjusting the dough with water or flour as necessary. Change to the dough hook and knead on medium-low speed until the dough is tacky, soft, and smooth, about 6 minutes. To make the dough by hand, stir the dry ingredients together with a whisk, then stir in the yeast mixture to make a sticky dough. Turn the dough out onto a floured work surface and knead, taking care not to add too much flour, until the dough is soft and smooth, about 8 minutes. Shape the dough into a ball.

3 Transfer the dough to a lightly oiled medium bowl. Turn to coat the dough with oil. Cover tightly with plastic wrap. Let stand in a warm place until almost doubled in volume, about 1½ hours.

4 Meanwhile, melt the butter in a small saucepan over medium heat. Remove from the heat and let stand for 3 minutes. Pour the clear liquid into a small bowl, leaving as much of the milky solids as possible in the saucepan.

5 Divide the dough into 12 equal pieces and shape each into a ball. Cover the balls loosely with plastic wrap. On a lightly floured surface, roll, pat, and stretch each ball into an oval about 6 in/15 cm long and 4 in/10 cm wide. Arrange the ovals, slightly overlapping, on a baking sheet.

6 Mix the green onions and garlic together in a small bowl. Heat a large, heavy skillet, preferably cast iron, over medium-high heat. Brush one side of an oval with melted butter. Place, buttered side down, in the skillet and cover. Cook until the underside is browned and the top is bubbled, about 1 minute. Turn the oval, brush with melted butter, scatter a generous sprinkle of the green onion mixture on top, and cook to brown the other side, about 1 minute more. Transfer to a platter lined with a large cloth napkin and cover with the napkin to keep warm. Repeat with the remaining ovals. Serve the naan warm or at room temperature.

MAKES 12 FLATBREADS

You may have noticed a "new" vegetable that looks like thin broccoli. Although it goes by the Italianate name of broccolini, it is actually a Japanese hybrid of Chinese broccoli, with less bitter cabbage flavor. This simple recipe uses the Chinese technique of sautéing seasonings in oil to make a sizzling condiment.

BROCCOLINI WITH CHILE-LEMON OIL

3 Tbsp vegetable oil

1½ lb/680 g broccolini

Kosher salt

Zest of 1 lemon, removed in strips with a vegetable peeler and julienned

One 1-in/2.5-cm piece peeled ginger, julienned

1 small fresh red chile, minced with seeds

1 Heat a wok or large skillet over medium-high heat. Add 1 Tbsp of the oil and heat until very hot but not smoking. Add the broccolini and ¼ cup/60 ml water. Cover and cook, stirring occasionally, until crisp-tender, about 3 minutes. Drain in a colander. Arrange the broccolini on a serving platter. Season to taste with salt.

2 Heat the wok over medium-high heat. Add the remaining 2 Tbsp oil and heat until very hot and shimmering. Add the lemon zest, ginger, and chile and cook, stirring almost constantly, until fragrant, about 30 seconds. Pour the mixture over the broccolini and serve.

MAKES 4 TO 6 SERVINGS

If you like dark-purple Mediterranean globe eggplant, you'll love the various Asian varieties, which are sweeter and less bitter. They come in many colors, including lavender and white stripes, and can be round like a softball or long like a sausage. This recipe pairs the elongated lavender Japanese variety with a deeply flavored black bean sauce, perfect for spooning over rice as a side dish or a vegetarian main course.

EGGPLANT IN BLACK BEAN SAUCE

SAUCE BASE

1½ tsp cornstarch

½ cup/120 ml chicken stock or canned reduced-sodium broth

2 Tbsp rinsed and crushed Chinese fermented black beans (see Glossary, page 211)

2 Tbsp Chinese rice wine or dry sherry

1½ Tbsp soy sauce

½ tsp light brown sugar

3 Tbsp vegetable oil

4 Japanese eggplants (about 1¼ lb/570 g), halved lengthwise, then crosswise into pieces about ½ in/12 mm wide

2 green onions, 1 finely minced and 1 thinly sliced (white and green parts)

1 Tbsp peeled and minced fresh ginger

2 garlic cloves, finely chopped

1 To make the sauce base: Sprinkle the cornstarch over the stock in a small bowl and stir to dissolve the cornstarch. Add the black beans, rice wine, soy sauce, and brown sugar and mix well.

2 Heat a very large skillet or wok over high heat. Add 2 Tbsp of the oil and heat the oil until it is very hot and shimmering. Add the eggplant and cook, stirring occasionally, until partially browned and just tender, 4 to 5 minutes. Transfer the eggplant to a platter.

3 Add the remaining 1 Tbsp oil to the skillet and heat. Add the minced green onion, the ginger, and garlic and stir until fragrant, about 15 seconds. Stir the sauce base to blend in the cornstarch, then stir it into the skillet and bring to a boil. Return the eggplant to the skillet and cook, stirring often, until coated with the sauce. Pour onto the platter, sprinkle with the sliced green onion, and serve.

MAKES 4 TO 6 SERVINGS

Hawaiians usually serve rice plain, so it acts as a foil to the other flavors on the plate or in the bowl. But there are times when you might care to gild the lily. This recipe adds green tea, ginger, and green peas to make a good thing better. It works best with fragrant rice such as jasmine or basmati, but any long-grain rice may be used. Very few Asian-Americans add salt to rice, so it is optional here.

GREEN TEA RICE WITH PEAS

1½ cups/315 g jasmine, basmati, or other long-grain rice

3 thin slices peeled fresh ginger

2 tsp whole-leaf green tea, such as gunpowder

1 tsp kosher salt (optional)

½ cup/80 g thawed frozen green peas

1 Bring 3 cups/720 ml water, the rice, ginger, tea, and salt, if using, to a boil in a small saucepan. Reduce the heat to low and tightly cover the saucepan. Cook until the rice is tender and has absorbed the liquid, about 18 minutes. Remove the saucepan from the heat.

2 Add the peas to the saucepan but do not stir them into the rice. Cover the saucepan again and let the rice stand for 5 minutes. Fluff the rice with a fork and serve hot.

MAKES 4 SERVINGS

The daily meals of Hawaiians are rich with Portuguese foods, from the linguiça sausage on their breakfast plates to these fluffy rolls at dinner, used to sop up the gravy that they love. You'll find these amazingly light rolls (also called *pão doce* or *massa sovada*) all over the Islands, and now on the mainland, too, and they make fantastic sandwiches.

PORTUGUESE SWEET BREAD ROLLS

DOUGH

½ cup/120 ml whole milk

1 Tbsp active dry yeast (see Note)

½ cup/100 g sugar

2 large eggs

4 Tbsp/55 g unsalted butter, melted and cooled

1¼ tsp fine sea salt

3 cups/420 g unbleached all-purpose flour, or as needed

GLAZE

1 large egg yolk

1 Tbsp whole milk

1 To make the dough: Bring the milk to a simmer in a small saucepan. Pour into the bowl of a stand mixer or a large bowl and let cool to warm (about 110°F/43°C), 5 to 10 minutes. Sprinkle in the yeast and let stand until the yeast softens, about 5 minutes. Stir to dissolve the yeast. Add the sugar, eggs, butter, and salt and mix with the paddle attachment or a wooden spoon.

2 If using a mixer, on low speed gradually add enough of the flour to make a soft dough that barely clears the sides of the bowl. Replace the paddle with the dough hook. Knead on medium-low speed, adding more flour as necessary to make a smooth and tacky dough, about 6 minutes. To make by hand, stir in enough flour to make a shaggy dough. Turn out the dough onto a floured work surface and knead, adding more flour as necessary, to make a smooth, tacky dough, about 10 minutes. Do not add too much flour, as the soft dough will firm up during rising.

3 Lightly butter a medium bowl. Shape the dough into a ball, put in the bowl, and turn to coat with butter, leaving the dough smooth side up. Cover with plastic wrap. Let stand in a warm place until doubled in volume, about 2 hours. (This rich dough takes a bit longer to rise than plain dough with less butter and sugar.)

4 Lightly butter a 9-in/23-cm round cake pan. Punch the dough down and turn out onto an unfloured work surface. Cut the dough into sixths. One at a time, shape each into a taut ball: Cup your hand over the dough with your palm barely touching the top. Quickly rotate your hand in a tight circle to roll the dough under your hand and shape it into a ball. Space the balls equidistant apart in the pan, with one ball in the center. Lightly cover the pan with plastic wrap. Let rise in a warm place until doubled in volume, about 45 minutes.

5 Position a rack in the center of the oven and preheat the oven to 350°F/180°C.

6 To make the glaze: Mix the yolk and milk together in a small bowl. Lightly brush the tops of the rolls with the glaze. Bake until the rolls are golden brown, 25 to 30 minutes. Let cool in the pan for 10 minutes. Remove the rolls from the pan and serve warm or cooled to room temperature.

MAKES 6 LARGE ROLLS

NOTE: Instant (also called bread-machine and quick-rising) yeast does not work well with this kind of egg-and-sugar-laden dough, so stick to the active dry variety.

In Hawaii, the ocean is ubiquitous. White-capped waves wash onto the beach, where you can savor the view or dive in, depending on your preference. The waves create a surfer's paradise. Those who snorkel beneath the waves are rewarded with displays of the brightly hued marine life that lives among the coral reefs ringing the islands. In winter, humpback whales ply the waters, sometimes breaching the surface for all to see. Scuba divers can hear the whales' plaintive songs from far away. Even the Islands' hillside communities remain in close touch with the sea. From nearly every perspective, water is part of the view, stretching far beyond the coastline to the horizon's edge.

Without water, there would be no life. In fact, this life-giving liquid makes up as much as 75 percent of our bodies. Among other things, it carries nutrients to our cells and to the plant life around us. In Hawaiian mythology, Kane was the god of fresh water, and Kanaloa was god of the ocean and all marine life. Kanaloa took on the form of a squid or octopus, sailing smoothly through the sea depths while he managed his realm.

As they did long ago, local fishermen still harvest the sea's riches. They deliver the freshest fish to Tommy Bahama's Island restaurants, where the chefs write their menus based on the catch of the day. Our most-loved specialties include Mahi Mahi with Macadamia Nut Crust and Papaya Salsa (page 115), Ahi Tuna with Lemongrass Crust and Sweet Chili–Mustard Sauce (page 127), and Togarashi-Sesame Snapper with Sake and Lime Sauce (page 121). With the help of this book, you can now make these dishes at home.

As you peruse these pages, imagine the sound of the sea. Throughout the Islands, we hear it gently roaring—its power apparent from the shore and even more so when we sail upon it. We can also smell the ocean. Its briny, moist sensation leaves a fresh, clean feeling in our nose and on our palate. This freshness gives water its purifying essence—a key component among Nature's four elements.

DESSERTS

Many favorite Hawaiian sweets have their roots in traditional American desserts, such as pies and cakes, that were brought to the Islands by missionaries at church-run schools. These Yankee staples were transformed into "local" treats with the use of tropical fruits and ingredients like coconut milk and sweet rice flour, as exemplified by two of our most popular signature desserts: Piña Colada Cake and Pineapple Crème Brûlée.

181 JELLY MALASADAS

182 CHOCOLATE BUTTER MOCHI

183 BUTTER MOCHI

184 SHAVE ICE WITH FRESH FRUIT SYRUPS

186 KONA COFFEE FLAN

189 MANGO, RASPBERRY, AND GINGER PIE

190 GUAVA AND CURRANT TEA CAKE

193 PASSION FRUIT CHIFFON TART

194 BANANA AND COCONUT CREAM MERINGUE PIE

197 MACADAMIA NUT AND CHOCOLATE TOFFEE

199 PIÑA COLADA CAKE

203 PINEAPPLE CRÈME BRÛLÉE

204 DOBASH CAKE

Go to just about any Hawaiian community event (church bazaar, street fair, school bake sale), and you will find a brisk business in these Portuguese fritters. They harken back to the time when it was easier to bring a pot of oil up to temperature than it was to build a fire in an oven. This is a smaller batch to make on a weekend morning for a hearty brunch.

JELLY MALASADAS

MALASADAS

¼ cup/60 ml whole milk, plus more as needed

2 Tbsp unsalted butter

1 Tbsp sugar

¾ tsp active dry yeast

2 Tbsp warm (about 110°F/43°C) water

1 large egg

1¾ cups/245 g unbleached all-purpose flour, plus more as needed

¼ tsp table salt

Vegetable oil, for deep-frying

COATING AND FILLING

⅓ cup/65 g sugar

⅛ tsp ground cinnamon

½ cup/125 g guava or your favorite flavor jelly

1 To make the malasadas: Bring the ¼ cup/60 ml milk, butter, and sugar to a simmer in a small saucepan over medium heat. Pour into a small bowl and let cool, stirring occasionally, until tepid, about 15 minutes.

2 Sprinkle the yeast over the warm water in a custard cup or ramekin and let stand for 5 minutes. Stir to dissolve the yeast. Add to the milk mixture with the egg and beat to combine.

3 Place the 1¾ cups/245 g flour and the salt in a food processor. With the machine running, add the milk mixture and process to make a soft, tacky dough that rides on top of the blade. If the dough feels too soft, add flour, 1 Tbsp at a time, and process briefly. If it feels too firm, add milk, 1 Tbsp at a time, and process briefly. Process the dough for 30 seconds. To make by hand, pour the milk mixture into a medium bowl. Gradually stir in enough of the flour to make a soft dough. Turn the dough out onto a floured work surface and knead, adding more flour as necessary, to make a soft, smooth dough, about 8 minutes.

4 Shape the dough into a ball and place in a buttered bowl. Turn the dough to coat with butter. Cover the bowl with plastic wrap. Let stand in a warm place until almost doubled in volume, about 1½ hours.

5 Punch down the dough. Turn it in the bowl to coat again with butter, cover with plastic wrap, and let stand again until almost doubled, about 45 minutes.

6 Line a large baking sheet with parchment or waxed paper. Punch the dough down and turn out onto an unfloured work surface. Cut the dough into 8 equal pieces. One at a time, shape each into a taut ball: Cup your hand over the dough with your palm barely touching the top. Quickly rotate your hand in a tight circle to roll the dough under your hand and shape it into a ball. Place on the baking sheet and cover loosely with plastic wrap.

7 Line another large baking sheet with brown paper or paper towels. Pour 3 in/7.5 cm oil into a large, heavy saucepan and heat over high heat to 350°F/180°C on a deep-frying thermometer. In batches without crowding, deep-fry the dough, turning once, until golden brown, about 3 minutes. Using a wire spider or a slotted spoon, transfer the malasadas to the paper-lined baking sheet and let cool slightly.

8 To coat and fill the malasadas: Whisk the sugar and cinnamon together in a small bowl. Fit a pastry bag with a nozzle tip (also called Bismarck) pastry tube or a plain pastry tube with a ½-in/12-mm-diameter tip. Fill the bag with the jelly. One at a time, insert the pastry tip into the center of a malasada and squeeze the bag to fill it with about 1 Tbsp of the jelly. Roll each malasada in the cinnamon sugar to coat. Serve warm or cooled to room temperature.

MAKES ABOUT 8 MALASADAS

Mochi are Japanese confections made from rice flour, and the classic ones are often shaped like fancy French bonbons. The Hawaiian rendition, more like a cross between a brownie and a pudding, is gluten-free. Usually eaten out-of-hand, these are also terrific with a dollop of whipped cream and a scattering of fresh raspberries, if you wish.

CHOCOLATE BUTTER MOCHI

½ cup/115 g cold unsalted butter, cut up

6 oz/170 g coarsely chopped bittersweet chocolate

One 14-oz/400-g can unsweetened coconut milk (not cream of coconut)

One 12-oz/340-g can evaporated milk

2 large eggs

2 tsp vanilla extract

2 cups/300 g sweet rice flour (mochiko)

1½ cups/300 g granulated sugar

¼ cup/25 g natural cocoa powder (not Dutch-processed)

1 Tbsp baking soda

1 tsp fine sea salt

Confectioners' sugar, for serving

WHIPPED CREAM

¾ cup/180 ml heavy cream

2 tsp confectioners' sugar

½ tsp vanilla extract

1 Position a rack in the center of the oven and preheat the oven to 350°F/180°C. Butter a 9-by-13-in/23-by-33-cm baking pan.

2 Melt the butter in a large saucepan over medium heat. Remove from the heat. Stir in the chocolate. Let the mixture stand until the chocolate softens, about 3 minutes. Whisk until the mixture is smooth. Add the coconut milk, evaporated milk, eggs, and vanilla and whisk until combined.

3 Sift the rice flour, granulated sugar, cocoa powder, baking soda, and salt together into a large bowl. Add to the chocolate mixture and whisk just until smooth. Spread evenly in the baking pan.

4 Bake until the mochi top is shiny and the batter feels barely set in the center when pressed gently with your fingertips, 50 to 55 minutes. Let cool completely in the pan on a wire rack. (The mochi can be covered and stored at room temperature for up to 3 days.)

5 To make the whipped cream: Using a hand mixer on high speed or a whisk, whip the ingredients together in a chilled medium bowl until stiff peaks form.

6 Cut the mochi into squares. Sift confectioners' sugar over the top and serve with the whipped cream.

MAKES 12 TO 15 SERVINGS

Many Hawaiian desserts are made with canned milk because fresh dairy products were not easy to come by in the past and they spoiled easily in the heat. In this recipe, the most common mochi, coconut milk and evaporated milk combine with sweet rice flour for a chewy, custard-like bar. If you are in the mood for more coconut, make the variation.

BUTTER MOCHI

One 1-lb/455-g box sweet rice flour (mochiko), about 3 cups

2¼ cups/450 g sugar

2 tsp baking powder

One 14-oz/400-g can unsweetened coconut milk (not cream of coconut)

One 12-oz/340-g can evaporated milk

5 large eggs

4 Tbsp/55g unsalted butter, melted

1 tsp vanilla extract

1 Position a rack in the center of the oven and preheat the oven to 350°F/180°C. Butter a 9-by-13-in/23-by-33-cm baking sheet.

2 Sift the rice flour, sugar, and baking powder together into a large bowl. Make a well in the center. Whisk the coconut milk, evaporated milk, eggs, melted butter, and vanilla until combined in another bowl. Pour into the well and stir until smooth. Spread evenly in the prepared pan.

3 Bake until the mochi feels just set in the center when pressed gently with your fingertips, 50 to 55 minutes. Let cool completely in the pan on a wire rack. Cut the mochi into squares and serve. (The mochi can be covered and stored at room temperature for up to 3 days.)

MAKES 12 TO 15 SERVINGS

COCONUT BUTTER MOCHI: Fold 1 cup/100 g sweetened coconut flakes into the finished batter.

Shave ice (there is no final *d* in this pidgin word) is a beloved Island treat. The best shops make their own syrups, and you can, too. Here are six syrups to prepare at home, each yielding about 2 cups/480 ml. You can find inexpensive home-model shave ice machines online. Some Islanders add a spoonful of sweetened red bean paste to the ice, or drizzle it with condensed milk.

SHAVE ICE WITH FRESH FRUIT SYRUPS

PASSION FRUIT, GUAVA, OR MANGO SYRUP

1 cup/200 g sugar

1 cup/240 ml thawed frozen passion fruit (also called *parcha* or *maracuya*), guava (*guayaba*), or mango purée

2 Tbsp fresh lemon juice, or as needed

PINEAPPLE, STRAWBERRY, OR CHERRY SYRUP

¾ cup/150 g sugar

2½ cups/475 g packed chopped fresh pineapple, 2 cups/280 g coarsely chopped fresh strawberries, or 2½ cups/375 g coarsely chopped unpitted fresh Bing cherries

2 Tbsp fresh lemon juice, or as needed

SPECIAL EQUIPMENT: Shave ice machine (see Note), plastic squeeze bottles with nozzles, straws

1 To make the passion fruit, guava, or mango syrup: Bring the sugar and 1 cup/240 ml water to a boil in a medium nonreactive saucepan over high heat, stirring to dissolve the sugar. Add the purée, return to a boil, and reduce the heat to medium-low. Simmer, stirring occasionally, until combined and slightly reduced, about 5 minutes. Transfer to a medium bowl and let cool completely. Adjust the sweetness with lemon juice.

2 To make the pineapple, strawberry, or cherry syrup: Bring the sugar and ¾ cup/180 ml water to a boil in a medium nonreactive saucepan over high heat, stirring to dissolve the sugar. Add the fruit with any juices (and cherry pits, if using), return to a boil, and reduce the heat to medium-low. Simmer, stirring occasionally, until the fruit is very tender and the syrup is slightly reduced, about 15 minutes. Strain through a sieve over a medium bowl, pressing hard on the solids with a wooden spoon. Discard the solids. Let the syrup cool completely. Adjust the sweetness with lemon juice.

3 Cover and refrigerate the syrup until chilled, at least 2 hours or up to 1 week. Before serving, transfer the syrup to a plastic squeeze bottle with a nozzle.

4 Following the machine directions, shave the ice into a bowl or decorative glass. Using the back of a large serving spoon, press and shape the ice into a dome. Squeeze about ½ cup/120 ml of the syrup over the ice, using the nozzle to squirt syrup to reach the bottom of the ice. Serve immediately with a spoon and a straw.

MAKES ABOUT 4 SERVINGS PER SYRUP, DEPENDING ON THE SIZE OF THE ICE SERVING

NOTE: Shave ice machines come in both hand-cranked and electric models. Some require freezing a block of ice to fit the machine, and others use ice cubes from your freezer. Just choose the one that works best with your lifestyle, keeping in mind that the molds for some brands will take up a fair amount of room in your freezer.

While Kona coffee is the most famous version of Hawaiian coffee, each island has a crop to call its own. Any of them will work in this cool, silky smooth dessert that is perfect for entertaining because it must be made ahead, leaving only the unmolding for serving. You will need six ¾-cup/180-ml ramekins for this recipe.

KONA COFFEE FLAN

CARAMEL

1 cup/200 g sugar

CUSTARD

1¼ cups/300 ml whole milk

1¼ cups/300 ml heavy cream

⅓ cup/30 g very coarsely ground medium-roast coffee beans, preferably Kona (ground in a coffee grinder or blender)

1 large egg, plus 5 large egg yolks

⅔ cup/130 g sugar

1 tsp vanilla extract

1 To make the caramel: Have ready six ¾-cup/180-ml ramekins. Bring the sugar and 3 Tbsp water to a boil in a small saucepan over high heat, stirring to dissolve the sugar. When the sugar boils, stop stirring and cook, occasionally swirling the pan by the handle, until the caramel is amber in color and very lightly smoking, about 5 minutes. (The caramel will read about 330°F/165°C on a candy or instant-read thermometer.) Carefully pour an equal amount of the caramel into each ramekin, quickly tilting and rotating the ramekin to coat the inside with caramel. Place the ramekins in a large roasting pan.

2 Position a rack in the center of the oven and preheat the oven to 325°F/165°C.

3 To make the custard: Bring the milk, cream, and ground coffee to a simmer in a heavy, medium saucepan over medium heat. Remove from the heat and let steep for 15 minutes. Strain the mixture through a fine-mesh sieve into a medium bowl, pressing hard on the solids.

4 Whisk the eggs, yolks, and sugar together in a medium bowl. Gradually whisk in the warm coffee mixture, followed by the vanilla. Strain the custard through the sieve into a 4-cup/960-ml measuring cup or pitcher. Pour and divide the custard evenly among the ramekins. Skim off any foam from each. Pour hot water into the roasting pan to come about one-third up the sides of the ramekins.

5 Bake until the custard seems set and doesn't jiggle when a ramekin is gently shaken, about 1 hour. Remove the flans from the roasting pan and let cool to room temperature. Wrap each flan with plastic wrap and refrigerate until chilled, at least 4 hours or up to 2 days.

6 For each serving, run a dinner knife around the inside of a ramekin to loosen the flan, being sure to reach the bottom of the ramekin to break the custard's suction. Cover with a dessert plate. Holding the plate and ramekin together, invert them and give them a strong shake to unmold the flan with its caramel. Serve chilled.

MAKES 6 SERVINGS

Solid American fare came to the Islands with the New England missionaries, and before long, pies were being made with the local tropical fruits. Here is one with the unexpected flavor of fresh ginger. Don't fight the urge to serve vanilla or macadamia nut ice cream with this.

MANGO, RASPBERRY, AND GINGER PIE

FILLING

6 ripe mangoes, pitted, peeled, and cut into ½-in/12-mm slices

¾ cup/150 g sugar

3 Tbsp instant tapioca, ground to a powder in a coffee grinder or blender

Grated zest of 1 lime

2 Tbsp fresh lime juice

2 Tbsp peeled and minced fresh ginger

12 oz/340 g fresh raspberries (2⅔ cups)

2 Tbsp unsalted butter, thinly sliced

Double-Crust Pastry Dough (page 195)

1 To make the filling: Toss the mangoes, sugar, tapioca, lime zest and juice, and ginger in a large bowl and let stand until the mangoes give off some juice, about 15 minutes. Gently mix in the raspberries and butter.

2 Position a rack in the bottom third of the oven and preheat the oven to 400°F/200°C. Heat a rimmed baking sheet in the oven.

3 Unwrap the dough. On a lightly floured work surface, roll out one disk of dough into a round about 13 in/33 cm in diameter and ⅛ in/3 mm thick. You should see flattened flakes of fat in the dough. Fit the dough into a 9-in/23-cm pie pan, preferably Pyrex. Trim the dough to a ⅛-in/3-mm overhang. Pour in the mango filling. On a lightly floured work surface, roll out the other disk of dough into a round 13 in/33 cm in diameter and ⅛ in/3 mm thick. Center the round over the filling. Trim the top crust to a ½-in/12-mm overhang. Tuck the top crust under the bottom crust and flute the edges. Cut a few slits in the top crust. Freeze or refrigerate the pie for 10 to 15 minutes.

4 Place the pie on the hot baking sheet. Bake for 15 minutes. Reduce the temperature to 350°F/180°C and continue baking until the crust is golden brown and the filling is bubbling, about 45 minutes. Transfer the pie to a wire rack and let cool completely, at least 3 hours. Cut into wedges and serve.

MAKES 8 TO 10 SERVINGS

This simple loaf has the unique tropical flavor of guava in every bite. It's not too sweet and even on the plain side, which makes it perfect with a cup of tea or coffee (perhaps brewed from one of the Hawaiian varieties). If you have fresh guavas, use them, but frozen guava purée works especially well, as does the banana variation.

GUAVA AND CURRANT TEA CAKE

1¾ cups/245 g unbleached all-purpose flour

2 tsp baking powder

¼ tsp baking soda

½ tsp salt

6 Tbsp/85 g unsalted butter, at room temperature

½ cup/100 g packed light brown sugar

¼ cup/50 g granulated sugar

2 large eggs, at room temperature

1 tsp vanilla extract

¾ cup/180 ml thawed frozen guava (*guayaba*) purée

½ cup/85 g dried currants or coarsely chopped dark raisins

ICING

1 cup/100 g confectioners' sugar

1 tsp fresh lemon juice

2 Tbsp whole milk, as needed

1 Position a rack in the center of the oven and preheat the oven to 350°F/180°C. Lightly butter an 8½-by-4½-in/21.5-by-11-cm loaf pan. Line the bottom with waxed paper. Dust with flour and tap out the excess.

2 Sift the flour, baking powder, baking soda, and salt into a medium bowl. Using a hand mixer on high speed or a wooden spoon, beat the butter in a large bowl until creamy. Gradually beat in the brown and granulated sugars and beat until the mixture is light in color and texture, about 3 minutes with a mixer or 5 minutes by hand. One at a time, beat in the eggs, mixing well after each addition, followed by the vanilla. Reduce the mixer speed to low. In thirds, alternating with two additions of the guava purée, mix in the flour mixture, scraping down the bowl as needed, just until the batter is smooth. Fold in the currants. Spread the batter evenly in the pan.

3 Bake until the loaf is golden brown and a bamboo skewer inserted in the center comes out clean, 50 to 60 minutes. Let cool for 10 minutes on a wire rack. Invert and unmold the loaf onto the rack and discard the waxed paper. Turn the loaf right side up and let cool completely.

4 To make the icing: Sift the confectioners' sugar into a small bowl. Add the lemon juice and stir in enough of the milk to make an icing with the consistency of thick cream.

5 Position a rimmed baking sheet beneath the cake on the rack. Pour the icing over the top of the cake, smoothing the icing with a metal spatula and allowing the excess to run down the sides of the cake. Let stand until the icing sets, about 1 hour. (The cake can be covered loosely with plastic wrap and stored at room temperature for up to 2 days.) Slice and serve.

MAKES 1 LOAF; SERVES 6 TO 8

BANANA-CHOCOLATE TEA CAKE: Every baker in the Islands has a family recipe for banana cake. Be sure to use ripe bananas with brown-speckled skins, not squishy black ones. Substitute ¾ cup/180 ml mashed ripe banana (about 2 large bananas) for the guava purée, and ½ cup/80 g miniature chocolate chips for the currants.

Passion fruit (called lilikoi in Hawaii), with its puckery surface, looks rather unpromising in the market. But cut one open, take a whiff of its perfumed scent, and you will be transported to an Island retreat. This is a tart to serve to company, with a buttery crust, a light and creamy filling, and a sweet-and-tangy drizzle of sauce the color of a Hawaiian sunset.

PASSION FRUIT CHIFFON TART

DOUGH

1 cup/140 g unbleached flour

3 Tbsp sugar

¼ tsp fine sea salt

6 Tbsp/85 g cold unsalted butter, cut into ½-in/12-mm cubes

1 large egg yolk

FILLING

½ cup/120 ml thawed frozen passion fruit (also called *maracuya* or *parcha*) purée

2 tsp unflavored gelatin

2 large eggs, separated, at room temperature

⅓ cup/65 g sugar

½ cup/120 ml heavy cream

SAUCE

⅔ cup/165 ml thawed frozen or fresh seeded passion fruit purée

3 Tbsp sugar, or more to taste

1 tsp cornstarch

1 Tbsp passion fruit liqueur or amber rum

1 recipe Whipped Cream (page 182)

1 Position a rack in the center of the oven and preheat the oven to 375°F/190°C.

2 To make the dough: Pulse the flour, sugar, and salt together in a food processor to combine, or stir them together in a medium bowl. Add the butter and pulse until the mixture resembles coarse meal with some pea-sized pieces of butter, or cut in the butter with a pastry blender. Add the yolk and pulse or stir until the dough clumps together. Gather the dough into a ball. Press the dough firmly and evenly into a 9-in/23-cm tart pan with a removable bottom; make sure the dough is not too thick in the corners of the pan. Pierce the dough all over with a fork. Freeze the dough for 15 minutes.

3 Line the dough with aluminum foil and fill with pie weights or dried beans. Bake until the dough is set and beginning to brown, about 15 minutes. Lift off the foil with the weights and continue baking until the crust is lightly browned, about 15 minutes more. Let the crust cool completely on a wire rack.

4 To make the filling: Pour the purée into a small saucepan and sprinkle the gelatin on top. Let stand until the gelatin softens, about 5 minutes. Cook over low heat, stirring constantly, until the mixture is hot but not boiling and the gelatin is completely dissolved. Remove from the heat.

5 Using a hand mixer on high speed or a whisk, beat the egg yolks and sugar in a medium bowl until the mixture is pale yellow and thick. Mix in the hot gelatin mixture. Place the bowl in a larger bowl of ice water and let stand, stirring often, until the mixture is cool and just beginning to thicken and set, about 5 minutes. Remove the bowl from the ice water, or the mixture will continue to set.

6 Using clean beaters, beat the egg whites with the mixer on high speed, or with a whisk, in a medium bowl until soft peaks form. Add the whites to the passion fruit mixture and whisk gently to combine. Whip the cream with the mixer or whisk until stiff peaks form, then gently whisk it into the passion fruit mixture until combined. Spread the filling in the cooled tart shell. Refrigerate until the filling is set, at least 2 or up to 24 hours.

7 To make the sauce: Bring the purée and sugar to a simmer in a small saucepan over low heat, stirring often. Taste for more sugar. Sprinkle the cornstarch over the liqueur in a custard cup and stir to dissolve. Stir into the purée and stir until it returns to a simmer and thickens. Pour into a small bowl. Let the sauce cool, then cover and refrigerate until chilled, at least 2 hours or up to 1 day.

8 Transfer the whipped cream to a pastry bag fitted with a ½-in/12-mm fluted pastry tip. Pipe the cream around the edges of the tart filling. Remove the sides of the tart pan. Slice and serve with the sauce.

MAKES 8 SERVINGS

The coconut, an iconic tropical fruit, is the basis for a whole slew of beloved desserts, and coconut cream pie is at the top of the list. This version adds bananas to the filling and is topped with meringue. A bit of cornstarch in the meringue stabilizes it to keep it from shrinking after baking.

BANANA AND COCONUT CREAM MERINGUE PIE

Pastry Dough (page 195)

FILLING

¾ cup/150 g sugar

¼ cup/30 g cornstarch

One 14-oz/400-g can coconut milk (not cream of coconut)

1 cup/240 ml plus 2 Tbsp whole milk

4 large egg yolks (save the whites for the meringue)

1 Tbsp unsalted butter

1 tsp vanilla extract

½ cup/50 g sweetened coconut flakes or desiccated coconut

MERINGUE

4 large egg whites, at room temperature

½ cup/100 g sugar

1 tsp cornstarch

2 bananas, thinly sliced

1 Position a rack in the bottom third of the oven and preheat the oven to 400°/200°C. Heat a rimmed baking sheet in the oven.

2 Unwrap the dough. On a lightly floured work surface, roll the dough into a round about 13 in/33 cm in diameter and ⅛ in/3 mm thick. You should see flattened flakes of fat in the dough. Fit the dough into a 9-in/23-cm pie pan, preferably Pyrex. Trim the overhanging dough to a ½-in/12-mm overhang. Fold the edge of the dough under so it is flush with the edge of the pan and flute the edges. Prick the dough all over with a fork. Freeze or refrigerate the pie crust for 10 to 15 minutes.

3 Line the dough with a sheet of aluminum foil. Fill the foil with pie weights or dried beans. Place the pan on the hot baking sheet and bake until the dough looks set and is beginning to brown, about 15 minutes. Remove the foil and weights. Continue baking, pricking the dough with a fork if it bubbles up, until crisp and golden brown, about 15 minutes more. Let cool completely on a wire rack.

4 To make the filling: Whisk the sugar and cornstarch together in a heavy, medium saucepan. Gradually whisk in the coconut milk and whole milk. Whisking almost constantly, cook over medium heat until the mixture comes to a simmer and thickens. Remove from the heat. Whisk the yolks together in a medium bowl to combine. Gradually whisk in about half of the hot milk mixture and return it to the saucepan. Bring to a full boil, whisking constantly, over medium heat, then cook for 30 seconds; the filling will have a pudding-like consistency. Strain the filling through a sieve into a clean medium bowl to remove any cooked bits of whites. Add the butter and vanilla and whisk until the butter melts. Press a sheet of plastic wrap directly onto the surface of the filling and pierce a few holes in the plastic with the tip of sharp knife. Let cool to room temperature. Stir in the coconut. Refrigerate until chilled, at least 2 hours.

5 To make the meringue: Position a rack in the center of the oven and preheat the oven to 350°F/180°C.

6 Beat the egg whites in a medium bowl with a hand-held electric mixer on high speed or with a whisk until soft peaks form. Mix the sugar and cornstarch together in a small bowl. Beat in the sugar mixture, 1 Tbsp at a time, and continue beating until the meringue forms stiff, glossy peaks.

7 Spread the bananas in the pie shell. Top with the filling and spread it evenly. Top with the meringue, making sure it touches the crust all around and swirling it into peaks with the back of a spoon. Bake until the meringue is peaked with brown, 3 to 5 minutes. Let cool completely. (The pie can be refrigerated for up to 1 day.) Cut into wedges and serve.

MAKES 8 TO 10 SERVINGS

Every baker has a favorite pie dough. Ours uses both shortening and butter, the former for flakiness and the latter for flavor. It also has a splash of vinegar to discourage gluten formation, which helps to keep the pastry tender. The dough is easiest to handle if refrigerated for an hour or so, but not chilled until hard.

Pastry Dough

1½ cups/210 g unbleached all-purpose flour

1 Tbsp sugar

¼ tsp salt

6 Tbsp/85 g cold vegetable shortening, cut into ½-in/12-mm cubes

3 Tbsp cold unsalted butter, cut into ½-in/12-mm cubes

¼ cup/60 ml ice-cold water

1 large egg yolk

½ tsp cider vinegar

1 **To make the dough:** Whisk the flour, sugar, and salt in a large bowl until combined. Add the shortening and butter. Using a pastry blender, rapidly cut the fats into the flour mixture until it is the consistency of coarse bread crumbs with some pea-sized pieces. Do not cut in the fats until the mixture has a uniform texture—the larger pieces of butter will make the baked crust flaky.

2 Whisk the cold water, yolk, and vinegar together in a liquid measuring cup. Gradually stir in enough of the water mixture into the flour mixture until the dough begins to clump together. You may not need all of the liquid. Gather the dough into a ball. Divide the dough in half and shape into thick disks. Wrap each disk in plastic wrap. Refrigerate just until chilled, about 1 hour. (The dough can be refrigerated for up to 1 day. If too hard to roll out, let it stand at room temperature for about 10 minutes to soften slightly.)

MAKES ONE 9-IN/23-CM CRUST

DOUBLE-CRUST PASTRY DOUGH: Use 2¼ cups/315 g flour, 1½ Tbsp sugar, ½ tsp salt, ½ cup/115 g plus 1 Tbsp cold vegetable shortening, 5 Tbsp/70 g cold unsalted butter, ⅓ cup/75 ml plus 1 Tbsp ice-cold water, 1 large egg yolk, and ¾ tsp cider vinegar. Divide the dough into 2 equal disks, wrap, and refrigerate.

The Hawaiian climate is not conducive to candy making, because humidity plays havoc with melted sugar. However, toffee is such a great showcase for buttery macadamia nuts that this recipe is worth including here. And homemade toffee is a fantastic gift at the holidays. The secret to perfect toffee is to stir it constantly during cooking.

MACADAMIA NUT AND CHOCOLATE TOFFEE

1 cup/225 g cold unsalted butter, cut into cubes

1½ cups/300 g sugar

3 Tbsp light corn syrup

¼ tsp fine sea salt

12 oz/340 g unsalted macadamia nuts, half finely chopped and half coarsely chopped

1 tsp vanilla extract

1 cup/170 g semisweet or milk chocolate chips

1 Line a large rimmed baking sheet with a silicone baking mat or lightly oil the baking sheet.

2 Combine the butter, sugar, corn syrup, 3 Tbsp water, and salt together in a heavy, medium saucepan. Attach a candy thermometer to the saucepan. Stirring constantly with a wooden spoon at a steady but not rapid pace, bring the mixture to a boil over medium heat. Continue cooking at medium heat, stirring constantly, until the mixture turns deep gold in color and registers 300°F/150°C on the thermometer, 12 to 15 minutes. If you stop stirring, the toffee may separate, so don't disregard this detail. Remove from the heat.

3 Add the finely chopped macadamia nuts and vanilla to the saucepan and stir gently to combine. Pour the mixture out onto the baking mat, letting it spread naturally. Let cool until set and warm, about 5 minutes. Sprinkle the chips evenly over the warm toffee. Let stand until the chips are softened and shiny, about 5 minutes. Using a flexible spatula, gently spread the chocolate evenly over the toffee. Sprinkle the coarsely chopped macadamia nuts over the chocolate. Let the toffee cool completely, at least 2 hours.

4 Break the toffee as desired into bite-size or larger chunks. Store in an airtight container at room temperature for up to 1 week.

MAKES ABOUT 1½ LB/680 G

This cake added to Tommy Bahama's reputation as a place to go for indulgent desserts with "tropical vacation" in their DNA. It consists of four layers of tender cake moistened with dark rum and filled with white chocolate mousse, crushed pineapple, and toasted coconut, then frosted with more mousse and coconut.

PIÑA COLADA CAKE

CAKE

¾ cup/170 g unsalted butter, at room temperature

1½ cups/300 g granulated sugar

2 cups/225 g cake flour

1 tsp baking powder

½ tsp baking soda

½ tsp fine sea salt

6 large egg whites

¾ cup/180 ml buttermilk

2 tsp vanilla extract

One 7-oz/200-g bag sweetened coconut flakes (2⅔ cups)

Two 20-oz/570-g cans crushed pineapple in juice

WHITE CHOCOLATE MOUSSE

3 cups/720 ml heavy cream

10 oz/280 g white chocolate, coarsely chopped, or 1⅔ cups/280 g white chocolate chips (see Note, page 200)

¼ cup/25 g confectioners' sugar

1 tsp vanilla extract

4 Tbsp/60 ml dark rum, such as Myers's

1 To make the cake: Position a rack in the center of the oven and preheat the oven to 350°F/180°C. Butter two 9-by-1½-in/23-by-4-cm round cake pans. Line the bottoms of the pans with waxed paper. Coat the pans with flour and tap out the excess flour.

2 Beat the butter in a large bowl with an electric mixer on high speed until creamy, about 1 minute. Gradually beat in the granulated sugar and continue beating, occasionally scraping down the sides of the bowl with a flexible spatula, until the mixture is light in color and texture, about 3 minutes.

3 Sift the flour, baking powder, baking soda, and salt together in a large bowl. Whisk the egg whites, buttermilk, and vanilla together in a medium bowl just to combine them. With the mixer on low speed, add the flour mixture in thirds, alternating with two equal additions of the buttermilk mixture, and mix, scraping down the bowl as needed, just until the batter is smooth. Divide the batter evenly among the cake pans and smooth the tops.

4 Bake until a wooden toothpick inserted into the center of the cakes comes out clean, about 30 minutes. Remove from the oven but keep the oven on. Let the cakes cool in the pan on wire racks for 10 minutes. Run a knife around the insides of the pans and invert and unmold the cakes onto the racks. Remove the paper and let cool completely.

5 Meanwhile, spread the coconut on a large rimmed baking sheet. Bake, stirring occasionally, until the coconut is toasted to golden brown, 12 to 15 minutes. Let cool completely.

6 Drain the pineapple well in a sieve. Squeeze the pineapple gently to remove its excess juice—you should have about 1½ cups/225 g pineapple.

7 To make the mousse: Heat 1 cup/240 ml of the cream in a small saucepan over medium heat until simmering. Put the white chocolate in a medium heat-proof bowl. Pour in the hot cream. Let the mixture stand for 3 minutes to soften the white chocolate and whisk until smooth. Let stand at room temperature until cool and thickened but still liquid, about 1 hour.

(continued)

PIÑA COLADA CAKE, continued

8 Chill a large bowl in the freezer or refrigerator. Add the remaining 2 cups/480 ml cream with the confectioners' sugar and vanilla. Whip with an electric mixer on high speed until the mixture forms soft peaks. Add the cooled white chocolate mixture. Using a large wire whisk (do not use the mixer), whip just until the mousse is combined and forms soft peaks again—do not overmix. The mousse will be soft, but spreadable. Set aside 1½ cups/360 ml of the mousse in a small bowl, cover, and refrigerate until serving.

9 Using a long serrated knife, cut each cake layer in half horizontally. Place one cake half, browned side down, on a cake platter. Slip strips of waxed paper under the cake to protect the platter during icing. Brush and drizzle 1 Tbsp of the rum over the cake. Spread with about ¾ cup/180 ml of the mousse, and evenly scatter about ½ cup/75 g of the pineapple on top. Repeat with two of the remaining cake layers. Top with the remaining cake layer, cut side up, brush with the remaining 1 Tbsp rum, and top with the remaining mousse. Using an icing spatula, frost the top and sides of the cake with the mousse. Don't worry if the mousse doesn't mask the cake completely, as it will be covered with coconut later. Refrigerate the cake until the mousse is cool and firm, at least 1 or up to 8 hours.

10 Working over a rimmed baking sheet, pat the coconut all over the top and sides of the cake, letting the excess coconut fall onto the baking sheet so it can be reapplied where necessary. Cover the cake loosely with plastic wrap and refrigerate until ready to serve, up to 1 day.

11 Let the cake stand at room temperature for about 1 hour before serving. Remove the waxed paper strips. Transfer the reserved mousse to a pastry bag fitted with a ½-in/12-mm star tip. Using a sharp knife, slice the cake. Pipe a large rosette of mousse next to each slice and serve.

MAKES 8 TO 10 SERVINGS

NOTE: When purchasing white chocolate, for the best results, check the label for a brand that contains cocoa butter and skip the brands with palm oil.

This spectacular dessert from Tommy's restaurants is so popular, we give out stacks of recipes every year. *Spectacular* is a strong word, but what else do you call bowls made from pineapple shells filled with caramelized fruit and custard, then topped with a thin sugar crust? It is surprisingly easy to pull off. You will need a butane kitchen torch for the brûlée topping.

PINEAPPLE CRÈME BRÛLÉE

PINEAPPLE AND FILLING

2 ripe pineapples

⅓ cup/65 g packed light brown sugar

½ tsp vanilla extract

CUSTARD

1½ cups/360 ml heavy cream

1 vanilla bean, halved lengthwise, or 1 tsp vanilla extract

6 large eggs, plus 6 large egg yolks

⅓ cup/65 g plus 1 Tbsp granulated sugar

9 tsp granulated sugar

Whipped Cream (page 182)

6 fresh strawberries, for garnish

SPECIAL EQUIPMENT: **Butane kitchen torch**

1 To prepare the pineapple shells: Slice off the bottom and crown of leaves from each pineapple. Using scissors, snip off and refrigerate 12 to 18 of the best-looking small pineapple leaves. Cut the pineapples crosswise into 6 rounds, each about 1½ in/4 cm thick. Do not peel the pineapple rounds. Reserve the remaining pineapple for another use. Cover and refrigerate the pineapple shells until serving.

2 For each shell, using a small, sharp knife, cut an incision about ¼ in/6 mm from the edge around the inside circumference of a pineapple round, being sure not to cut all the way through to the bottom. Using a melon baller, scoop out and discard the central core, leaving about ¼ in/6 mm of fruit on the bottom of the shell. Scoop out the pineapple within the incision, leaving a shell about ¼ in/6 mm thick. Finely chop the pineapple flesh. You should have 2 cups/380 g. Transfer the chopped pineapple to a medium bowl and stir in the brown sugar.

3 Heat a large nonstick skillet over medium-high heat. Add the pineapple mixture and cook, stirring occasionally, until the juices have evaporated and the pineapple is browned, 8 to 10 minutes. Return to the bowl and let cool completely. Stir in the vanilla. Cover and refrigerate until chilled, at least 4 hours or up to 1 day.

4 To make the custard: Bring the heavy cream and vanilla bean halves to a simmer in a heavy, medium saucepan over medium heat. Remove from the heat and let steep for 5 minutes. Using the tip of a small, sharp knife, scrape the seeds from the bean halves into the cream, discarding the bean halves. Whisk the eggs, yolks, and granulated sugar together in a medium heat-proof bowl. Gradually whisk in the hot cream mixture. Return to the saucepan. Cook over low heat, stirring constantly, until the mixture is thick enough to coat a wooden spoon (your finger should leave a path in the custard) and an instant-read thermometer reads 185°F/85°C. Do not boil. Pour the custard through a sieve into a heat-proof bowl. (Stir in the vanilla extract now, if using.) Let cool completely. Cover with plastic wrap and refrigerate until chilled and thickened, at least 4 hours or up to 1 day.

5 Divide the pineapple mixture evenly among the pineapple shells, spreading it evenly. Place the rounds on a baking sheet. Spoon equal amounts of the custard into each round and smooth the custard with a small spatula. Cover each with a piece of waxed or parchment paper and refrigerate until serving, at least 1 or up to 4 hours.

6 To serve: Sprinkle each custard evenly with 1½ tsp granulated sugar. Using the torch, wave the flame about ½ in/12 mm above the custard to caramelize the sugar. Fill a pastry bag fitted with a ½-in/12-mm fluted tip with the whipped cream. Pipe a large rosette of whipped cream onto each custard and insert 2 or 3 pineapple leaves into each rosette. Garnish each with a strawberry. Serve immediately.

MAKES 6 SERVINGS

Many an American baker has returned from a trip to Hungary inspired by the famous Dobos torta, even if the spelling and ingredients are reinterpreted. (In New Orleans, it is called doberge cake.) In Hawaii, a couple of local bakeries made it a specialty, and now dobash cake, its chocolate layers held together with a soft, pudding-textured frosting, is the cake of choice for many celebrations.

DOBASH CAKE

CAKE

1½ cups/190 g cake flour

1½ cups/300 g sugar

⅓ cup/35 g plus 1 Tbsp natural cocoa powder (not Dutch-processed)

¾ tsp baking soda

¾ tsp salt

1 cup/240 ml whole milk

3 large eggs, separated, at room temperature

⅓ cup/75 ml vegetable oil

FROSTING

1 cup/200 g sugar

½ cup/50 g natural cocoa powder (not Dutch-processed)

⅓ cup/40 g cornstarch

¼ tsp salt

2 tsp instant espresso or regular instant coffee

1½ cups/360 ml hot water

½ cup/120 ml heavy cream

4 Tbsp/55 g unsalted butter

1 tsp vanilla extract

1 To make the cake: Position a rack in the center of the oven and preheat the oven to 350°F/180°C. Lightly butter two 8-in/20-cm round cake pans with 2-in/5-cm sides. Line the bottoms with parchment or waxed paper rounds. Dust the insides of the pans with flour and tap out the excess.

2 Sift the cake flour with 1 cup/200 g of the sugar, the cocoa, baking soda, and salt together into a medium bowl. Whisk the milk, egg yolks, and oil together in a small bowl. Pour into the flour mixture and mix with an electric mixer on medium speed, scraping down the sides of the bowl as needed, until the batter is smooth. Using clean beaters, beat the egg whites with an electric mixer on high speed until soft peaks form. Gradually beat in the remaining ½ cup/100 g of the sugar until stiff, glossy peaks form. Fold into the batter. Divide the batter among the cake pans. (The batter will be on the thin side.)

3 Bake until the cakes begin to shrink away from the sides of the pans, about 30 minutes. Let cool in the pans on wire racks for 10 minutes. Invert and unmold the cakes onto the wire racks and remove the paper. Turn the cakes right side up and let cool completely.

4 To make the frosting: Whisk the sugar, cocoa, cornstarch, and salt together in a heavy, medium saucepan. Dissolve the espresso in the hot water. Gradually whisk the coffee mixture into the saucepan, followed by the cream. Bring to a boil over medium heat, whisking constantly, making sure that the whisk reaches into the corners of the saucepan. Remove from the heat. Add the butter and vanilla and whisk until smooth.

5 Scrape the frosting into a medium bowl set in a larger bowl of ice water. Let stand, stirring often, until the frosting is cool and firm enough to spread, about 10 minutes. Remove the bowl of frosting from the ice water.

6 Using a serrated knife, trim and level the tops of the cakes. Place one cake, cut side down, on a cake platter. Slip strips of waxed paper under the cake to protect the platter from frosting. Spread about ¾ cup/180 ml of the icing over the layer. Top with the second layer, cut side up. Spread the top, and then the sides, of the cake with the frosting. This frosting is soft, but firms up as it is spread. Let the frosting set, about 30 minutes. (The cake can be refrigerated, uncovered, for up to 1 day. Remove from the refrigerator about 30 minutes before serving.) Remove the paper strips. Slice and serve the cake.

MAKES 8 TO 10 SERVINGS

GREENWELL
FARMS
KONA COFFEE
Kealakekua, HI

Tom Greenwell starts each day with a freshly brewed cup of Kona coffee from his family's Greenwell Farms. He takes his first cup with a little cream and sugar. "The best thing about being a coffee grower is having the best cup of coffee in the world every morning," Tom says.

Founded in 1850 by Tom's great-grandfather, Henry Greenwell, Greenwell Farms was mainly a cattle ranch until 1985. Henry's wife, Elizabeth, planted some coffee plants there in the early days, and some of them are still alive today.

Tom was raised on the ranch, where he was known as the Mechanic. Apparently, he could fix anything. "When my father decided to change our main interest from cattle to coffee in 1985," Tom recalls, "I thought I'd be moving on to do something else. But my dad had a different idea. He told me I was going to stay on the ranch, even though he had no money to pay me! So we jumped into it, and it was great."

After his father passed away in 1992, Tom took over. "We farm to keep the ecosystem in top shape," he says. "On our mountainous slopes, ground cover is important for erosion control. We also use a lot of organic methods to promote a healthy soil. In fact, we have a full-time biologist on our staff."

Hawaii is the only state in the United States where coffee is grown. "The Kona region has a terrain conducive to growing coffee and not much else," Tom explains. "It produces a smooth, mild, and flavorful drink without bitterness." After his first cup, this farmer drinks his coffee black. "I've been known to drink 10 to 12 cups a day," he says with pride. "Some people say that's too much. But you can't drink too much good coffee!"

GREENWELL FARMS, KEALAKEKUA

GLOSSARY

The intriguing flavors of Hawaiian foods are a gift from the cultures of Japan, China, the Philippines, Thailand, Vietnam, Portugal, and even Yankee America. The ethnic ingredients that define this cuisine are widely available for purchase on the mainland at Asian and Latino grocers, many supermarkets, and online.

Shopping at your local ethnic market will likely be a fascinating experience that can provide you with a new source for fresh produce, seafood, spices, and sauces. Most Asian seasonings keep indefinitely after opening in the refrigerator or a cool, dark place, so it is worth stocking up. Also, you may find your own creative uses for some of these ingredients, such as stirring hoisin sauce or Korean *gochugaru* into ketchup for a quick barbecue sauce, or seasoning sandwiches or sauces with Sriracha. Discovering the umami properties of fish sauce, miso, and mirin could change your everyday cooking.

BANANA LEAVES: These huge leaves are sold folded and frozen in large plastic packages at Asian and Latino markets. They thaw quickly, and can be cut to size as needed.

BASIL, THAI: A member of the basil family used in Thai cooking. Its dark-green leaves have a spicier flavor than the Italian variety, which can be used as a substitute.

BLACK BEANS, CHINESE: You will find small bags of these soft, fermented and salted beans at Asian grocers. Rinse the salt off before using. Store the beans in a jar to keep their pungent aroma at bay.

BLACK VINEGAR: Fermented from a single ingredient (such as rice, millet, or wheat) or a combination, this dark Chinese vinegar has a smoky flavor a little like that of balsamic vinegar, which can be substituted.

CHILES, DRIED: Many Chinese-American dishes, such as General Tso's chicken, get their kick from dried chiles. In Asian markets, these are usually bagged as "dried chili peppers," but in spice stores, look for the *tien tsin* variety. About 3 in/7.5 cm long, these are a dark brick-red color. They are usually fried whole, seeds and all, to flavor the cooking oil in a recipe.

CHILES, FRESH: In our recipes, we use the small, red (and very hot) Thai chile as our all-purpose fresh chile. Only about 1 in/2.5 cm long, the ripe red chile has a slightly sweeter flavor than the green one. Because the seeds contain the greatest concentration of capsaicin, the compound that puts the heat in chiles, many cooks remove the seeds before cooking. This is difficult to do with such small ones, though, so just mince them, seeds and all, and use them according to your heat tolerance.

CHORIZO, SMOKED: A smoked, moderately spicy hard Portuguese or Spanish sausage used in Filipino cooking. Do not confuse it with the soft, unsmoked Mexican version.

COCONUT MILK: Sold canned and unsweetened. Be sure to shake the can well before using, and take care to choose coconut milk, not cream; this highly sweetened ingredient is used mainly in cocktails.

CURRY PASTE, THAI: Sold in jars or cans, there are three main kinds: red (with a base of red chiles), green (made with cilantro and fresh chiles), and yellow (which blends Indian spices with garlic, lemongrass, and other seasonings). Leftover curry paste can be covered tightly and refrigerated for up to 1 month.

CURRY POWDER, MADRAS: India has a wide variety of curry powders, but this familiar all-purpose kind has a good dose of turmeric to give it a golden color and relatively mild flavor.

DOENJANG: A Korean soybean paste similar to miso but stronger, saltier, and chunkier. You can use *aka miso* as a substitute.

FISH SAUCE, THAI OR VIETNAMESE: Made from fermented anchovies, this thin, salty seasoning is sold at most supermarkets in the Asian section. The Thai (*nam pla*) and Vietnamese (*nuoc mam*) versions are very similar, and interchangeable in recipes. Tiparos and Squid are reliable brands.

FRUIT PURÉE, FROZEN: Latino markets carry high-quality frozen tropical fruit purées—Goya is a popular brand. Flavors include passion fruit (also labeled *maracuya*), guava (*guayaba*), tamarind, mango, and papaya.

FURIKAKE: This Japanese seasoning mixture has a base of dried seaweed flakes flavored with sesame seeds and other ingredients. There are many varieties (wasabi, dried fish, and dried miso), but *fumi nori* is the most versatile. It is most often used as a topping for rice, and as a component of musubi.

GOCHUGARU: Korean red chili flakes used in making kimchi. Be sure to get the flakes and not the powdered or shredded kind.

GOCHUJANG: A thick red Korean chili paste, made from fermented chiles, soybeans, and rice. For an inauthentic but tasty substitute for *gochujang*, use 2 or 3 canned chipotle chiles in adobo, finely minced into a paste. The chipotles won't supply the same bulk, but the spiciness level is similar.

GYOZA WRAPPERS: Round dumpling wrappers, found in the refrigerated section of many supermarkets.

HOISIN SAUCE: An intensely flavored thick mixture of soybeans, chiles, and seasonings, this sauce is sweet, salty, and spicy at the same time.

JÍCAMA: Spanish explorers brought this tuber from Mexico to the Philippines, and from there it spread throughout Asia. Sold at specialty foods markets and many supermarkets, its crunchy texture is great in slaws, salads, and even stir-fries.

KAMABOKO: This cooked fish paste molded into a loaf shape is often called fish cake in Hawaii. The most common kind in the Islands has a pink and white spiral pattern. It is very similar to surimi (imitation crab sticks), which can be sliced and used as a substitute, as can cooked shrimp.

KIAWE: Native to Hawaii, this very hard wood is the preferred wood for grilling in Hawaii. It is usually sold in chunks, not chips, and is available online from hawaiiguava.com. Mesquite, found at supermarkets and hardware stores on the mainland, is a great substitute.

LEMONGRASS: A fragrant, somewhat hard rhizome used in Southeast Asian cooking to lend a citrusy aroma and flavor to food. It must be minced to be edible, although sometimes a stalk of lemongrass is steeped in hot broth as a flavoring. Peel off the outer layer to expose the inner white bulb. Using a large knife, chop off the tough stem top. The tender bulb part can now be minced by hand, or first coarsely chopped with a large knife and then minced in a food processor.

LINGUIÇA: The most common Portuguese sausage. Smoked and sliceable, it is seasoned with vinegar, garlic, and paprika. Smoked chorizo is the best substitute, or use any smoked hard sausage, including kielbasa.

LO MEIN: Chinese egg noodles, available fresh or dried in Chinese markets and the Asian section of some specialty foods stores.

MIRIN: A sweet Japanese rice wine used in cooking, available in both domestic and imported brands. Look for naturally fermented *hon-mirin* at Asian markets. The supermarket variety (*aji-mirin*) is artificially sweetened, although it will do.

MISO: A Japanese fermented bean paste with a complex, salty taste, miso is sold at natural foods stores as well as Asian markets and many supermarkets. The three basic varieties are white (*shiro*, young, mild, and pale in color), yellow (*shinsu*, moderately aged and flavored, and dark beige in color), and red (*aka*, well aged, strongly flavored, and dark-brown in color).

MOCHIKO: Milled from mochi rice, this Japanese sweet rice flour is found in Asian markets (look for the domestic Blue Star brand) or in supermarkets in the gluten-free or baking aisle. *Mochiko* gives baked goods a tender crumb and is often used in deep-frying batters because it does not absorb liquid as readily as wheat flour. Sweet rice flour does not contain sugar; the name is just a way to identify it from other rice flours.

NORI: Squares of dried seaweed used in making sushi and musubi. Be sure to buy the toasted version, clearly labeled on the package, which has a crisper texture. If necessary to toast, quickly wave the seaweed over an open flame (a gas burner or grill) until it turns a darker shade of green—this may take only a few seconds. Let cool before using.

OYSTER SAUCE: Thick and earthy, this Chinese seasoning sauce has pureed oysters as its main ingredient.

PANCIT: In Filipino cooking, *pancit* refers to any kind of noodle. We use *pancit canton* (yellow flour noodles) on page 147; Japanese *chuka soba* are a good substitute. Do not confuse these with *pancit bihon*, which are rice noodles, similar to the kind used for pad Thai.

PANKO: Japanese bread crumbs. Flakier and coarser than the American version, these create a light, crunchy coating. Once considered exotic, they can now be found at any supermarket.

RAMEN: Curly wheat noodles sold dried or fresh, usually in individual servings with seasoning packets. (You will have no need for the seasoning packets.) Ramen are deep-fried, which gives them an especially firm and chewy texture. Look for fresh ramen in the refrigerated or frozen section of Asian markets.

RICE FLOUR: See *mochiko*.

RICE VINEGAR: Fermented from rice wine, this vinegar is known for its mild acidity and rounded flavor. There are two versions, so look closely at the label. We always use unseasoned rice vinegar. Seasoned rice vinegar has salt and sugar to flavor warm rice for sushi.

RICE WINE, CHINESE: Also called Shaoxing rice wine, it is available at Asian markets with liquor departments and liquor stores in Chinese neighborhoods. Look for the Pagoda brand. Other than in California and some other states without state-operated liquor stores, most markets can legally sell only salted "cooking wine," which should be avoided. Dry sherry is a time-honored substitute.

SAIMIN NOODLES: These thin, egg noodles are made with wheat flour and are sold fresh or dried at Hawaiian grocers, but away from the Islands, cooks will have to make do with substitutes. Fresh or dried Chinese egg noodles are the best substitute, or use thin linguine.

SAKE: This rice-based alcoholic beverage is actually brewed, so it is not a wine. For cooking, use a reasonably priced *junmai*-style sake sold in large bottles, such as Gekkeikan brand. After opening, this kind of sake can be refrigerated for 2 to 3 months. (In general, the best sake for drinking is sold in small bottles and should be consumed soon after opening.)

SALT, HAWAIIAN PINK: The pink clay known as *alaea* colors this solar-dried sea salt, giving the flakes a slightly more complex mineral flavor. While you can use pink salt for everyday cooking (and may substitute it for the kosher salt called for in this book), it is especially good as a finishing salt, added to the food just before serving so its coarse texture and color remain intact. Black Hawaiian salt is also a great finishing salt, but the pulverized black volcanic charcoal is added to the salt flakes and does not occur naturally.

SAUSAGE, CHINESE: These sausages are thinner, shorter, and sweeter than many dried sausages. There really isn't a substitute, but you could use diced prosciutto (which is similar to Chinese ham) to provide some pork flavor to a dish.

SESAME OIL, ASIAN: This oil is used as a nutty seasoning, and never for sautéing, as it burns at much lower temperatures than other oils. The sesame seeds are toasted before processing to give the oil a deeper flavor. This differentiates it from clear, expeller-pressed sesame oil, which has little taste.

SHIITAKE MUSHROOMS, DRIED: Chinese cooks often prefer the chewier texture of soaked dried mushrooms to fresh ones. Many supermarkets now carry dried shiitakes in the produce section with a selection of other dried mushrooms. Dried shiitakes should be soaked in hot water for 20 to 30 minutes until softened. To cut the soaking time by about half, put the mushrooms in a microwave-safe bowl, cover with cold water, and microwave on high until the liquid comes to a boil, about 2 minutes. Drain the mushrooms, discarding the liquid. Trim away any tough stems left on the caps. Some recipes call for fresh shiitake mushrooms. When you use them, be sure to discard the inedible stem before cutting up the cap.

SOBA: A good all-purpose Japanese dried noodle that is usually made with buckwheat. Versions with a high proportion of wheat flour can stand in for *saimin* and ramen. The fresh version sold at Asian markets is almost invariably buckwheat soba.

SOY SAUCE: In Hawaii, soy sauce is called *shoyu*. Some local brands (such as Aloha) have a lighter body and less salty flavor than Japanese and Chinese varieties. We use Japanese soy sauce (such as Kikkoman) because it is readily available on both the mainland and in the Islands. It is made with both soybeans and wheat for a rounded taste, whereas the Chinese sauce is usually fermented from soy alone.

SRIRACHA SAUCE: A very hot fermented chili sauce, familiar to most mainlanders in the red squeeze bottle with a rooster on the label, although imported brands (also called Sriracha) are sold in Asian markets.

TAMARIND CONCENTRATE: Fresh tamarind is hard to use, as its tart pulp is encased in a barklike pod. Tamarind concentrate, made from the cleaned and reduced pulp, is much more convenient. You'll find it in Asian and Indian markets in a plastic container.

TIGER LILY BUDS, DRIED: Golden brown lily buds are essential to traditional hot and sour soup (page 50) and are sold at Asian markets. They must be soaked in hot water to soften, then drained before using.

TOGARASHI, SHICHIMI: Another Japanese seasoning you'll find yourself sprinkling with abandon on your food, *shichimi togarashi* is a spicy mixture of seven spices and seasonings. As with *furikake*, there are several different kinds of *togarashi*, but the *shichimi* variety, with red chiles, dried orange peel, and sesame seeds, is the most common and versatile.

WASABI POWDER: This pale-green powder of dried wasabi needs to be constituted into a paste with water before using. A dash of vinegar helps to fix the heat level, which otherwise dissipates.

WOOD EAR MUSHROOMS, DRIED: Also called tree mushrooms, these thin, floppy translucent fungi may be found in their fresh form in some specialty foods stores, but Asian markets sell the dried variety. Soak them in hot water to soften, then drain and rinse well to remove any grit.

ACKNOWLEDGMENTS

The combined efforts of several individuals have allowed us to offer *Flavors of Aloha* for your home kitchen.

We thank esteemed writers Rick Rodgers and Jeff Morgan for their invaluable contributions to this project. Our thanks to the photography team of Peden + Munk for inspired and gorgeous photos both in the studio and on location in Hawaii, and to designer Toni Tajima for making the pages and text look beautiful. Thank you to the creative prop and food styling team led by Amy Wilson and Alison Attenborough, assisted by Julian Bolton, Petericia Ellis, Nina Lalli, Dan Rosenzweig, and Hadas Smirnoff, and as well to photo assistant Jaesung Lee and digital technician William Joos.

We are grateful to the producers and growers on the Island who welcomed us into their unique operations and offered insights and personal stories: thank you Tom Greenwell of Greenwell Farms, Royce Hirayama and Stennis Hirayama of Hirayama Farms, fisherman Alan Kiriu, Steve Sakala of Honaunau Farm, and Parker Ranch and cow boss Keoki Wood.

We value the efforts of our own team members in making this endeavor productive and successful. Thank you and congratulations to: Rachel Dawson, Don Donley, Rob Goldberg, Stennis Hirayama, Eric Karp, Kouri Killmeier, Shannon Mills, Terry R. Pillow, Thomas Prowell, Ferdinand van Alphen, and Kyle Zitek.

We appreciate the opportunity to collaborate with Chronicle Books, and our thanks to the fine team assembled to produce this book: Mike Ashby, Pamela Geismar, Catherine Huchting, Tera Killip, Laurel Leigh, Carolyn Miller, and Beth Weber.

And to our customers and readers of this book, our continued thanks for keeping us inspired and motivated. We sincerely hope that you enjoy cooking with Tommy Bahama.

INDEX

A

Adobo, Pork, 96
Ahi Tuna with Lemongrass Crust and Sweet Chili–Mustard Sauce, 127
Arugula, Fruit, and Goat Cheese Salad with Papaya Vinaigrette, 54
Asian Chicken Broth, 149
Asian Slaw with Ginger Dressing, 58
Asparagus
 Asparagus with Oyster Sauce, 168
 Sweet and Sour Chicken with Mango and Asparagus, 80
Avocados
 Avocado Wasabi Cream, 25
 Guacamole, 25

B

Bacon
 Chicken and Bacon Empanadas, 79
 Fried Rice with Kimchi, Bacon, and Peas, 141
 Maui Sweet Onion, Bacon, and Chive Dip, 33
 Pork Burgers with Pineapple Chutney and Bacon, 108
Bamboo shoots
 Pork Ramen with Shoyu Broth, 150
 Tom Yum Shrimp Soup, 51
Bananas
 Banana and Coconut Cream Meringue Pie, 194
 Banana-Chocolate Tea Cake, 190
Bánh Mì, Grilled Chicken, 85
Bartending tools, 28
Beach, Donn, 22, 75
Bean, Red, and Ham Soup, 48
Bean sprouts
 Chinatown Chow Mein with Pork and Mushrooms, 143
 Tom Yum Shrimp Soup, 51
 Vietnamese Noodle Soup with Beef, 144
Beef. *See also* Cattle ranches
 Grilled Skirt Steaks with Kona Coffee Rub, 102
 Grilled Tamarind Short Ribs, 89
 Korean Steak with Ssamjang Dip, 90
 Ono Oxtail and Greens Soup, 45
 Paniolo Beef and Vegetable Stew, 105
 Vietnamese Noodle Soup with Beef, 144
Bergeron, "Trader Vic," 22, 167
Blue Hawaii, 29
Bok choy
 Braised Baby Bok Choy with Macadamia Nuts, 162
 Ono Oxtail and Greens Soup, 45
Bourbon
 Tropical Itch, 61
Braised Baby Bok Choy with Macadamia Nuts, 162
Braised Pork Belly in Steamed Buns, 92–93
Brandy
 Singapore Sling, 167
Bread. *See also* Sandwiches
 Braised Pork Belly in Steamed Buns, 92–93
 Green Onion and Garlic Naan, 169
 Portuguese Sweet Bread Rolls, 176
Broccolini with Chile-Lemon Oil, 170
Broths
 Asian Chicken Broth, 149
 Shoyu Broth, 150
Buns, Steamed, Braised Pork Belly in, 92–93
Burgers, Pork, with Pineapple Chutney and Bacon, 108
Butter Mochi, 183

C

Cabbage
 Asian Slaw with Ginger Dressing, 58
 Cabbage and Daikon Kimchi, 158
 Grilled Pineapple Asian Slaw, 58
 Pan-Cooked Noodles with Shrimp and Chorizo (*Pancit*), 147
 Red Bean and Ham Soup, 48
Cakes
 Banana-Chocolate Tea Cake, 190
 Dobash Cake, 204
 Guava and Currant Tea Cake, 190
 Piña Colada Cake, 199–200
Caramel Sauce, 76
Carrots
 Carrot-Miso Dressing, 59
 Korean Cellophane Noodles with Chicken and Vegetables, 136
 Ono Oxtail and Greens Soup, 45
 Paniolo Beef and Vegetable Stew, 105
 Pickled Vegetables, 85
 Red Bean and Ham Soup, 48
 Spicy Sake Pickles, 39
Cataplana, 128
Cattle ranches, 88, 105, 113, 207
Cellophane Noodles, Korean, with Chicken and Vegetables, 136
Cheese
 Arugula, Fruit, and Goat Cheese Salad with Papaya Vinaigrette, 54
 Chicken and Bacon Empanadas, 79
Cherries
 Cherry Blossom Martini, 29
 Cherry Syrup, 184
Chicken
 Asian Chicken Broth, 149
 Chicken and Bacon Empanadas, 79
 Chicken Chow Fun with Sugar Snap Peas and Shiitakes, 135
 Chicken Katsu with Umami Sauce, 68
 Chicken Teriyaki with Grilled Shiitake Mushrooms, 71
 Chicken Yakitori, 72
 Fried Chicken Mochiko, 83
 General Tso's Chicken, 67
 Grilled Chicken Bánh Mì, 85
 Korean Cellophane Noodles with Chicken and Vegetables, 136
 Kung Pao Chicken, 82
 Mandarin Hot and Sour Soup, 50
 Minced Chicken in Lettuce Cups, 35
 Roasted Korean Chicken Wings, 30
 Shoyu Broth, 150
 Sweet and Sour Chicken with Mango and Asparagus, 80
 Vietnamese Chicken Breasts with Savory Caramel Sauce, 76
Chinatown Chow Mein with Pork and Mushrooms, 143
Chinese Roast Duck with Orange-Honey Glaze, 73

Chocolate
Banana-Chocolate Tea Cake, 190
Chocolate Butter Mochi, 182
Dobash Cake, 204
Macadamia Nut and Chocolate Toffee, 197
Chow Fun, Chicken, with Sugar Snap Peas and Shiitakes, 135
Chow Mein, Chinatown, with Pork and Mushrooms, 143
Chutney, Pineapple, 108
Citrus and Hearts of Palm Salad with Kumquat Vinaigrette, 57
Clams
Clam Soup with Shiitakes and Miso, 46
Portuguese Seafood and Sausage Stew, 128
Cocktails
Blue Hawaii, 29
Cherry Blossom Martini, 29
equipment for making, 28
From-Scratch Sour Mix, 167
garnishes for, 28
Hibiscus Fizz, 138
Hibiscus Lime Cooler, 138
Mai Tai, 167
Painkiller No. 2, 75
Pineapple Plantation, 61
Singapore Sling, 167
tips for, 28
Tropical Itch, 61
Zombie, 75
Coconut
Banana and Coconut Cream Meringue Pie, 194
Coconut Butter Mochi, 183
Piña Colada Cake, 199–200
Tommy's Famous Coconut Shrimp, 22
Coconut milk
Banana and Coconut Cream Meringue Pie, 194
Butter Mochi, 183
Chocolate Butter Mochi, 182
Coconut Butter Mochi, 183
Lamb Shanks and Snap Peas with Red Curry Sauce, 100
Pork Satay with Peanut Sauce, 34
Shrimp and Scallops in Thai Curry Sauce, 116
Coffee, 102, 207
Grilled Skirt Steaks with Kona Coffee Rub, 102
Kona Coffee Flan, 186
Cointreau
Hibiscus Lime Cooler, 138
Mai Tai, 167
Tropical Itch, 61
Zombie, 75
Crab Rangoon, 21
Cream, Whipped, 182
Crème Brûlée, Pineapple, 203
Crispy Sriracha Shrimp, 26
Crosby, Bing, 29
Cucumbers
Spicy Sake Pickles, 39
Curaçao
Blue Hawaii, 29
Currant Tea Cake, Guava and, 190

D

Daikon
Cabbage and Daikon Kimchi, 158
Grilled Chicken Bánh Mì, 85
Pickled Vegetables, 85
Desserts
Banana and Coconut Cream Meringue Pie, 194
Banana-Chocolate Tea Cake, 190
Butter Mochi, 183
Chocolate Butter Mochi, 182
Coconut Butter Mochi, 183
Dobash Cake, 204
Guava and Currant Tea Cake, 190
Jelly Malasadas, 181
Kona Coffee Flan, 186
Macadamia Nut and Chocolate Toffee, 197
Mango, Raspberry, and Ginger Pie, 189
Passion Fruit Chiffon Tart, 193
Piña Colada Cake, 199–200
Pineapple Crème Brûlée, 203
Shave Ice with Fresh Fruit Syrups, 184
Dipping Sauce, 36
Dips
Maui Sweet Onion, Bacon, and Chive Dip, 33
Ssamjang Dip, 90
Direct heat, 19
Dobash Cake, 204
Double-Crust Pastry Dough, 195
Drunken Mushrooms, 160
Duck, Chinese Roast, with Orange-Honey Glaze, 73

E

Earth, 43
Eggplant in Black Bean Sauce, 172
Eggs
Garlic Fried Rice with Sausage, Eggs, and Green Onions, 142
Pork Ramen with Shoyu Broth, 150
Saimin with Asian Chicken Broth, 149
Empanadas, Chicken and Bacon, 79

F

Fire, 133
Fish, 17, 114, 179. *See also Kamaboko*
Ahi Tuna with Lemongrass Crust and Sweet Chili–Mustard Sauce, 127
Grilled Swordfish with Orange-Miso Marinade, 124
Lomi-Lomi Salmon with Tomatoes and Onions, 27
Mahi Mahi with Macadamia Nut Crust and Papaya Salsa, 115
Salmon Fillets with Ginger Glaze, 123
Steamed Sea Bass with Ginger Dipping Sauce, 118
Togarashi-Sesame Snapper with Sake and Lime Sauce, 121
Tuna Poke with Guacamole and Flatbread, 25
Flan, Kona Coffee, 186
Fried Chicken Mochiko, 83
Fried Rice with Kimchi, Bacon, and Peas, 141
From-Scratch Sour Mix, 167

G

Garlic
Garlic Fried Rice with Sausage, Eggs, and Green Onions, 142
Green Onion and Garlic Naan, 169
roasting, 161
Wasabi–Roasted Garlic Mashed Potatoes, 161
Wine and Garlic Marinade, 97
General Tso's Chicken, 67
Gin
Singapore Sling, 167
Ginger
Ginger Dipping Sauce, 118
Ginger Dressing, 58
Salmon Fillets with Ginger Glaze, 123
Grapefruit
Citrus and Hearts of Palm Salad with Kumquat Vinaigrette, 57
Spiced Grapefruit Syrup, 75

Green onions
Garlic Fried Rice with Sausage, Eggs, and Green Onions, 142
Green Onion and Garlic Naan, 169
Panko-Crusted Rack of Lamb with Green Onion Hoisin, 107
Green Papaya and Shrimp Salad, 53
Greens Soup, Ono Oxtail and, 45
Green Tea Rice with Peas, 175
Greenwell, Henry, 207
Greenwell, Tom and Elizabeth, 207
Greenwell Farms, 207
Grilled Chicken Bánh Mì, 85
Grilled Pineapple Asian Slaw, 58
Grilled Skirt Steaks with Kona Coffee Rub, 102
Grilled Swordfish with Orange-Miso Marinade, 124
Grilled Tamarind Short Ribs, 89
Grilling tips, 19
Guacamole, 25
Guava
Guava and Currant Tea Cake, 190
Guava-Glazed Baby Back Ribs, 94
Guava Syrup, 184
Gyoza, Pork and Shrimp, 36

H

Haleakala, Mount, 33, 133
Ham Soup, Red Bean and, 48
Hawaiian-Style Rice, 157
Hibiscus flowers
Hibiscus Fizz, 138
Hibiscus Lime Cooler, 138
Hibiscus Syrup, 138
Hina, 43
Hirayama, Royce and Stennis, 65
Hirayama Farms, 65
Honaunau Farm, 155
Hot and Sour Soup, Mandarin, 50
Huli Huli Pork Tenderloin and Pineapple with Old-School Teriyaki Marinade, 101

I

Imu, 19, 133
Indirect heat, 19

J

Jelly Malasadas, 181
Jícama
Asian Slaw with Ginger Dressing, 58
Grilled Pineapple Asian Slaw, 58

K

Kalua Pulled Pork Sandwiches, 99
Kamaboko (Japanese fish cake)
Pork Ramen with Shoyu Broth, 150
Saimin with Asian Chicken Broth, 149
Kamehameha III, King, 105
Kanaloa, 179
Kane, 43, 179
Kiawe, 99
Kilauea, 133
Kimchi
Cabbage and Daikon Kimchi, 158
Fried Rice with Kimchi, Bacon, and Peas, 141
Kiriu, Alan, 17
Kona Coffee Flan, 186
Korean Cellophane Noodles with Chicken and Vegetables, 136
Korean Steak with Ssamjang Dip, 90
Ku, 43
Kumquat Vinaigrette, 57
Kung Pao Chicken, 82

L

Lamb
Lamb Shanks and Snap Peas with Red Curry Sauce, 100
Panko-Crusted Rack of Lamb with Green Onion Hoisin, 107
Lemongrass
Ahi Tuna with Lemongrass Crust and Sweet Chili–Mustard Sauce, 127
Tom Yum Shrimp Soup, 51
Lettuce
Citrus and Hearts of Palm Salad with Kumquat Vinaigrette, 57
Minced Chicken in Lettuce Cups, 35
Romaine Hearts with Maui Onions and Carrot-Miso Dressing, 59
Limes
Hibiscus Lime Cooler, 138
Togarashi-Sesame Snapper with Sake and Lime Sauce, 121
Lomi-Lomi Salmon with Tomatoes and Onions, 27
Lono, 43

M

Macadamia nuts
Braised Baby Bok Choy with Macadamia Nuts, 162
Macadamia Nut and Chocolate Toffee, 197
Mahi Mahi with Macadamia Nut Crust and Papaya Salsa, 115
Macaroni Salad, Plate Lunch Potato-, 62
Mahi Mahi with Macadamia Nut Crust and Papaya Salsa, 115
Mai Tai, 167
Malasadas, Jelly, 181
Mandarin Hot and Sour Soup, 50
Mangoes
Mango, Raspberry, and Ginger Pie, 189
Mango Syrup, 184
Sweet and Sour Chicken with Mango and Asparagus, 80
Maraschino liqueur
Cherry Blossom Martini, 29
Marinades
Old-School Teriyaki Marinade, 101
Orange-Miso Marinade, 124
Wine and Garlic Marinade, 97
Martini, Cherry Blossom, 29
Maui (demigod), 133
Maui Sweet Onion, Bacon, and Chive Dip, 33
Mauna Loa, 133
Mayonnaise, Sriracha, 108
Minced Chicken in Lettuce Cups, 35
Miso
Carrot-Miso Dressing, 59
Clam Soup with Shiitakes and Miso, 46
Orange-Miso Marinade, 124
Mochi
Butter Mochi, 183
Chocolate Butter Mochi, 182
Coconut Butter Mochi, 183
Mousse, White Chocolate, 199–200
Mushrooms
Chicken Chow Fun with Sugar Snap Peas and Shiitakes, 135
Chicken Teriyaki with Grilled Shiitake Mushrooms, 71
Chinatown Chow Mein with Pork and Mushrooms, 143
Clam Soup with Shiitakes and Miso, 46
Drunken Mushrooms, 160
Korean Cellophane Noodles with Chicken and Vegetables, 136
Mandarin Hot and Sour Soup, 50
Minced Chicken in Lettuce Cups, 35
Mustard
Pineapple Mustard, 21
Sweet Chili–Mustard Sauce, 127
Musubi, Spam, 40

N

Naan, Green Onion and Garlic, 169
New Hawaiian Cuisine, 115, 161
Noodles
 Chicken Chow Fun with Sugar Snap Peas and Shiitakes, 135
 Chinatown Chow Mein with Pork and Mushrooms, 143
 Korean Cellophane Noodles with Chicken and Vegetables, 136
 Pan-Cooked Noodles with Shrimp and Chorizo (*Pancit*), 147
 Plate Lunch Potato-Macaroni Salad, 62
 Pork Ramen with Shoyu Broth, 150
 Saimin with Asian Chicken Broth, 149
 Vietnamese Noodle Soup with Beef, 144

O

Old-School Teriyaki Marinade, 101
Onions. *See also* Green onions
 Lomi-Lomi Salmon with Tomatoes and Onions, 27
 Maui Sweet Onion, Bacon, and Chive Dip, 33
 Romaine Hearts with Maui Onions and Carrot-Miso Dressing, 59
Ono Oxtail and Greens Soup, 45
Oranges
 Chinese Roast Duck with Orange-Honey Glaze, 73
 Citrus and Hearts of Palm Salad with Kumquat Vinaigrette, 57
 From-Scratch Sour Mix, 167
 Orange-Miso Marinade, 124
Orgeat, 167
Oxtail and Greens Soup, Ono, 45

P

Painkiller No. 2, 75
Paka'a, 87
Palm, Hearts of, and Citrus Salad with Kumquat Vinaigrette, 57
Pan-Cooked Noodles with Shrimp and Chorizo (*Pancit*), 147
Paniolo Beef and Vegetable Stew, 105
Panko-Crusted Rack of Lamb with Green Onion Hoisin, 107
Papaya
 Arugula, Fruit, and Goat Cheese Salad with Papaya Vinaigrette, 54
 Green Papaya and Shrimp Salad, 53
 Papaya Salsa, 115
Parker, John Palmer, 113
Parker Ranch, 105, 113
Passion fruit
 Passion Fruit Chiffon Tart, 193
 Passion Fruit Syrup, 184
 Tropical Itch, 61
Pastry Dough, 195
Peanuts
 Kung Pao Chicken, 82
 Ono Oxtail and Greens Soup, 45
 Peanut Sauce, 34
Peas
 Chicken Chow Fun with Sugar Snap Peas and Shiitakes, 135
 Fried Rice with Kimchi, Bacon, and Peas, 141
 Green Tea Rice with Peas, 175
 Lamb Shanks and Snap Peas with Red Curry Sauce, 100
 Pan-Cooked Noodles with Shrimp and Chorizo (*Pancit*), 147
Pho, 144
Pickles
 Cabbage and Daikon Kimchi, 158
 Pickled Vegetables, 85
 Spicy Sake Pickles, 39
Pie dough
 Double-Crust Pastry Dough, 195
 Pastry Dough, 195
Pies
 Banana and Coconut Cream Meringue Pie, 194
 Mango, Raspberry, and Ginger Pie, 189
Piña Colada Cake, 199–200
Pineapple
 Blue Hawaii, 29
 Grilled Pineapple Asian Slaw, 58
 Hibiscus Lime Cooler, 138
 Huli Huli Pork Tenderloin and Pineapple with Old-School Teriyaki Marinade, 101
 Mai Tai, 167
 Painkiller No. 2, 75
 Piña Colada Cake, 199–200
 Pineapple Chutney, 108
 Pineapple Crème Brûlée, 203
 Pineapple Mustard, 21
 Pineapple Plantation, 61
 Pineapple Syrup, 184
 Singapore Sling, 167
 Zombie, 75
Plate Lunch Potato-Macaroni Salad, 62
Poke, Tuna, with Guacamole and Flatbread, 25
Pork. *See also* Bacon; Sausage
 Braised Pork Belly in Steamed Buns, 92–93
 Chinatown Chow Mein with Pork and Mushrooms, 143
 Guava-Glazed Baby Back Ribs, 94
 Huli Huli Pork Tenderloin and Pineapple with Old-School Teriyaki Marinade, 101
 Kalua Pulled Pork Sandwiches, 99
 Mandarin Hot and Sour Soup, 50
 Pork Adobo, 96
 Pork and Shrimp Gyoza, 36
 Pork Burgers with Pineapple Chutney and Bacon, 108
 Pork Ramen with Shoyu Broth, 150
 Pork Satay with Peanut Sauce, 34
 Red Bean and Ham Soup, 48
 Roast Pork and Potatoes with Wine and Garlic Marinade, 97
 Saimin with Asian Chicken Broth, 149
 Spam Musubi, 40
Portuguese Seafood and Sausage Stew, 128
Portuguese Sweet Bread Rolls, 176
Potatoes
 Paniolo Beef and Vegetable Stew, 105
 Plate Lunch Potato-Macaroni Salad, 62
 Red Bean and Ham Soup, 48
 Roast Pork and Potatoes with Wine and Garlic Marinade, 97
 Wasabi–Roasted Garlic Mashed Potatoes, 161
Presley, Elvis, 29

R

Ramen, Pork, with Shoyu Broth, 150
Raspberry, Mango, and Ginger Pie, 189
Red Bean and Ham Soup, 48
Rice
 Fried Rice with Kimchi, Bacon, and Peas, 141
 Garlic Fried Rice with Sausage, Eggs, and Green Onions, 142
 Green Tea Rice with Peas, 175
 Hawaiian-Style Rice, 157
 Spam Musubi, 40
Rice flour
 Butter Mochi, 183
 Chocolate Butter Mochi, 182
 Coconut Butter Mochi, 183
 Fried Chicken Mochiko, 83
Roasted Korean Chicken Wings, 30

Roast Pork and Potatoes with Wine and Garlic Marinade, 97
Rolls, Portuguese Sweet Bread, 176
Romaine Hearts with Maui Onions and Carrot-Miso Dressing, 59
Rum
  Blue Hawaii, 29
  Mai Tai, 167
  Painkiller No. 2, 75
  Tropical Itch, 61
  Zombie, 75

S

Saimin with Asian Chicken Broth, 149
Sakala, Steve, 155
Sake
  Chicken Yakitori, 72
  Spicy Sake Pickles, 39
  Togarashi-Sesame Snapper with Sake and Lime Sauce, 121
Salad dressings
  Carrot-Miso Dressing, 59
  Ginger Dressing, 58
  Kumquat Vinaigrette, 57
  Papaya Vinaigrette, 54
Salads
  Arugula, Fruit, and Goat Cheese Salad with Papaya Vinaigrette, 54
  Asian Slaw with Ginger Dressing, 58
  Citrus and Hearts of Palm Salad with Kumquat Vinaigrette, 57
  Green Papaya and Shrimp Salad, 53
  Grilled Pineapple Asian Slaw, 58
  Plate Lunch Potato-Macaroni Salad, 62
  Romaine Hearts with Maui Onions and Carrot-Miso Dressing, 59
Salmon
  Lomi-Lomi Salmon with Tomatoes and Onions, 27
  Salmon Fillets with Ginger Glaze, 123
Sandwiches
  Grilled Chicken Bánh Mì, 85
  Kalua Pulled Pork Sandwiches, 99
  Pork Burgers with Pineapple Chutney and Bacon, 108
Satay, Pork, with Peanut Sauce, 34
Sauces
  Caramel Sauce, 76
  Dipping Sauce, 36
  Ginger Dipping Sauce, 118
  Papaya Salsa, 115
  Peanut Sauce, 34
  Sweet Chili–Mustard Sauce, 127
  Umami Sauce, 68
Sausage
  Garlic Fried Rice with Sausage, Eggs, and Green Onions, 142
  Pan-Cooked Noodles with Shrimp and Chorizo (*Pancit*), 147
  Portuguese Seafood and Sausage Stew, 128
  Red Bean and Ham Soup, 48
Scallops and Shrimp in Thai Curry Sauce, 116
Sea Bass, Steamed, with Ginger Dipping Sauce, 118
Sesame and Ginger Spinach, 165
Shave Ice with Fresh Fruit Syrups, 184
Shoyu Broth, 150
Shrimp
  Crispy Sriracha Shrimp, 26
  Green Papaya and Shrimp Salad, 53
  Pan-Cooked Noodles with Shrimp and Chorizo (*Pancit*), 147
  Pork and Shrimp Gyoza, 36
  Portuguese Seafood and Sausage Stew, 128
  Shrimp and Scallops in Thai Curry Sauce, 116
  Tommy's Famous Coconut Shrimp, 22
  Tom Yum Shrimp Soup, 51
Simple Syrup, 29
Singapore Sling, 167
Slaws
  Asian Slaw with Ginger Dressing, 58
  Grilled Pineapple Asian Slaw, 58
Snapper, Togarashi-Sesame, with Sake and Lime Sauce, 121
Soups
  Clam Soup with Shiitakes and Miso, 46
  Mandarin Hot and Sour Soup, 50
  Ono Oxtail and Greens Soup, 45
  Red Bean and Ham Soup, 48
  Saimin with Asian Chicken Broth, 149
  Tom Yum Shrimp Soup, 51
  Vietnamese Noodle Soup with Beef, 144
Sour Mix, From-Scratch, 167
Spam Musubi, 40
Spiced Grapefruit Syrup, 75
Spicy Sake Pickles, 39
Spinach
  Korean Cellophane Noodles with Chicken and Vegetables, 136
  Sesame and Ginger Spinach, 165
Sriracha Mayonnaise, 108
Ssamjang Dip, 90
Steamed Sea Bass with Ginger Dipping Sauce, 118
Strawberries
  Arugula, Fruit, and Goat Cheese Salad with Papaya Vinaigrette, 54
  Strawberry Syrup, 184
Sweet and Sour Chicken with Mango and Asparagus, 80
Sweet Chili–Mustard Sauce, 127
Swordfish, Grilled, with Orange-Miso Marinade, 124
Syrups
  Cherry Syrup, 184
  Guava Syrup, 184
  Hibiscus Syrup, 138
  Mango Syrup, 184
  Passion Fruit Syrup, 184
  Pineapple Syrup, 184
  Simple Syrup, 29
  Spiced Grapefruit Syrup, 75
  Strawberry Syrup, 184

T

Tamarind Short Ribs, Grilled, 89
Tart, Passion Fruit Chiffon, 193
Tea cakes
  Banana-Chocolate Tea Cake, 190
  Guava and Currant Tea Cake, 190
Tea Rice, Green, with Peas, 175
Teriyaki Marinade, Old-School, 101
Tiger lily buds
  Mandarin Hot and Sour Soup, 50
Ti leaves, 99
Toffee, Macadamia Nut and Chocolate, 197
Tofu
  Mandarin Hot and Sour Soup, 50
Togarashi-Sesame Snapper with Sake and Lime Sauce, 121
Tomatoes
  Lomi-Lomi Salmon with Tomatoes and Onions, 27
  Portuguese Seafood and Sausage Stew, 128
  Red Bean and Ham Soup, 48
  Romaine Hearts with Maui Onions and Carrot-Miso Dressing, 59
  Tom Yum Shrimp Soup, 51
Tommy's Famous Coconut Shrimp, 22
Tom Yum Shrimp Soup, 51

Triple sec
Hibiscus Lime Cooler, 138
Mai Tai, 167
Tropical Itch, 61
Zombie, 75
Tropical Itch, 61
Tuna
Ahi Tuna with Lemongrass Crust and Sweet Chili–Mustard Sauce, 127
Tuna Poke with Guacamole and Flatbread, 25
Two-zone cooking, 19

U

Umami Sauce, 68

V

Vietnamese Chicken Breasts with Savory Caramel Sauce, 76
Vietnamese Noodle Soup with Beef, 144
Vodka
Blue Hawaii, 29
Cherry Blossom Martini, 29
Hibiscus Lime Cooler, 138
Pineapple Plantation, 61
Volcanoes, 133

W

Wasabi
Avocado Wasabi Cream, 25
Wasabi–Roasted Garlic Mashed Potatoes, 161
Water, 179
Water chestnuts
Mandarin Hot and Sour Soup, 50
Minced Chicken in Lettuce Cups, 35
Whipped Cream, 182
Whiskey
Hibiscus Fizz, 138
Tropical Itch, 61
White chocolate
Piña Colada Cake, 199–200
purchasing, 200
White Chocolate Mousse, 199–200
Wind, 87
Wine and Garlic Marinade, 97
Wood, Keoki, 113

Y

Yee, Harry, 29

Z

Zombie, 75